CHENG & TSUI

"Bringing Asia to the World"™

中文听说读写 · 中文聽說讀寫

INTEGRATED CHINESE

Simplified and Traditional Characters

4

Workbook

4th Edition

Yuehua Liu and Tao-chung Yao
Liangyan Ge, Yaohua Shi, Nyan-Ping Bi

Original Edition by Yuehua Liu and Tao-chung Yao
Nyan-Ping Bi and Yaohua Shi

CHENG & TSUI

"Bringing Asia to the World"™

Copyright © 2019, 2010, 2006, 1997
Cheng & Tsui Company, Inc.

Fourth Edition

22 21 20 19 18   1 2 3 4 5

ISBN 978-1-62291-152-3 [Fourth Edition,
Simplified and Traditional Characters]

Printed in the United States of America

The *Integrated Chinese* series includes
textbooks, workbooks, character
workbooks, teacher's resources, streaming
audio, video, and more. Content is available
in a variety of formats, including print and
online via the ChengTsui Web App™. Visit
chengtsui.co for more information on the
other components of *Integrated Chinese*.

Publisher
JILL CHENG

Editors
RANDY TELFER, MIKE YONG and
LEI WANG

Creative Director
CHRISTIAN SABOGAL

Interior Design
LIZ YATES

Illustrators
KATE PAPADAKI with LIZ YATES

Photographs
© Adobe Stock
© Cheng & Tsui

Cheng & Tsui Company, Inc.
25 West Street
Boston, MA 02111-1213 USA
chengtsui.co
Phone (617) 988-2400 / (800) 554-1963
Fax (617) 426-3669

Contents

Preface

In designing the workbook exercises for Volumes 3 and 4 of *Integrated Chinese* (IC), we sought to give equal emphasis to the core language skills of listening, speaking, reading, and writing. For the new edition, we have also added *pinyin* and tone exercises for students to progressively improve their pronunciation and lesson opener checklists for them to track their learning. Where appropriate, we have labeled the exercises as interpretive, interpersonal, or presentational according to the American Council on the Teaching of Foreign Languages (ACTFL) *21st Century Skills Map for World Languages*.

In addition to the print editions, the IC workbooks are also available online through the **ChengTsui Web App™** (*Essential* and *Educator Editions*). In the digital format, the exercises are presented alongside the textbook content, and automatic feedback for students is provided. For more information about the Web App, visit chengtsui.co.

Organizational Principles

As with the textbooks, the IC Volume 3 and 4 workbooks do not follow one pedagogical methodology, but instead blend several effective teaching approaches. In addition, the full text is offered in both simplified and traditional characters, with simplified characters listed first. When accessed through the ChengTsui Web App, the workbooks are particularly suited for differentiated instruction, blended learning, and the flipped classroom. Here are some features that distinguish the IC workbooks:

Form and Function
The ultimate purpose of learning any language is to be able to communicate in that language. With that goal in mind, we pay equal attention to language form and function. In addition to traditional workbook exercise types (e.g., fill-in-the-blanks, sentence completion, translation, multiple choice), we include task-based assignments that equip students to handle real-life situations using accurate and appropriate language. These exercises provide linguistic context and are written to reflect idiomatic usage.

Visual Learning
Engaging learners through rich visuals is key to our pedagogy. To build a bridge between the classroom and the target language setting, we include a range of exercises centered on authentic materials. We also include illustration-based exercises that prompt students to answer questions directly in Chinese without going through the process of translation.

Learner-Centered Tasks
We believe that workbook exercises should not only align with the textbook, but also relate to students' lives. We include exercises that simulate daily life and reference culturally relevant topics and themes, including social media and globalization. We hope such open-ended exercises will actively engage students in the subject matter, and keep them interested in the language-learning process.

Differentiated Instruction
We have designed the exercises at different difficulty levels to suit varying curricular needs. Therefore, teachers should assign the exercises at their discretion; they may use some or all of them, in any sequence. Moreover, teachers may complement the workbook exercises with their own materials.

Bringing It Together
Every five lessons, we provide a short cumulative review unit ("Bringing It Together") for students who wish to check their progress. These flexible units do not introduce any new learning materials, and can be included in or excluded from curricula according to individual needs.

The exercises in this workbook have been designed to recycle vocabulary learned and provide a contextualized language environment.

The workbook lesson sections are as follows:

Listening Comprehension

All too often, listening comprehension is sacrificed in the formal classroom setting. Because of time constraints, students tend to focus their time and energy on mastering a few grammar points. We include a substantial number of listening comprehension exercises to remedy this imbalance. There are two categories of listening exercises; both can be done on students' own time or in the classroom. In either case, the instructor should review students' answers for accuracy.

The first group of listening exercises, which is placed at the beginning of this section, is based on the scenarios in the lesson. For the exercises to be meaningful, students should study the vocabulary list before listening to the recordings.

The second group of listening exercises is based on audio recordings of two or more short dialogues or narratives. These exercises are designed to give students extra practice on the vocabulary and grammar points introduced in the lesson. The Workbook Listening Rejoinder exercises are significantly more difficult than others. These exercises should be assigned towards the end of the lesson, after students have familiarized themselves with its content. For the Fourth Edition, these exercises have largely been reworked as multiple-choice or true/false questions to facilitate easy assessment.

Audio for the workbooks (and textbooks) is accessible via the ChengTsui Web App and, for print users, at chengtsui.co/resources.

Pinyin and Tone

To solidify students' grasp of the finer points of Mandarin pronunciation, this section incorporates exercises that focus specifically on comparing and distinguishing initials, finals, and tones, as well as on differentiating characters that have more than one pronunciation.

Speaking

As with Listening Comprehension, this section includes two groups of exercises. They should be assigned separately based on students' proficiency level.

To help students apply new vocabulary and grammar knowledge to meaningful communication, we first ask questions related to the Lesson Text, and then ask questions related to their own lives. These questions require a one- or two-sentence answer. By stringing together short questions and answers, students can construct their own dialogues, practice in pairs, or take turns asking or answering questions.

As their confidence increases, students can progress to more difficult prompts that invite them to express opinions on a number of topics. Some of these topics are abstract, so they gradually teach students to express their opinions in longer conversations or statements. As the school year progresses, these speaking exercises should take up more class discussion time. Because this second group of exercises can be challenging, it should be attempted only after students are well grounded in the lesson's grammar and vocabulary. Usually, this does not occur immediately after students have completed the first group of exercises.

Reading Comprehension

To help students understand how their newly acquired vocabulary and grammatical structures function in meaningful contexts, this section includes questions asking students to match terms, answer questions in English or Chinese, or answer multiple-choice questions based on readings. There are also activities based on realia. There are two types of reading exercises in the workbook: short passages incorporating new vocabulary and grammar structures from the lesson, and authentic materials such as advertisements, personal ads, and short news articles.

Writing and Grammar

As the culmination of each lesson, this section includes exercises that enable students to consolidate what they have just learned.

While training students to work on their proficiency at the sentence and paragraph levels, we saw a need to help students solidify their foundation in character recognition and word association. Hence, character- and word-building exercises are included in each lesson.

Open-ended prompts and exercises are provided to solidify students' grasp of important grammar points. Through brief exchanges, students answer questions using specific grammatical forms, or are given sentences to complete. Because they must provide context for these exercises, students cannot treat them as simple mechanical repetition drills.

Translation has been an age-old tool for language teaching and still has its place today. Positive student feedback confirms our belief in its continued importance. The translation exercises we have devised serve two primary functions: one, to have students apply specific grammatical structures; and two, to encourage students to build their vocabulary. Ultimately, we believe this dual-pronged approach will enable students to realize that it takes more than just literal translation to convey an idea in a foreign language.

We have also included exercises that encourage students to express themselves through writing. Many of the topics overlap with those used in oral practice, and we expect that students will find it easier to write what they have already learned to express orally.

Finally, to train students to tell a complete story based on what they see and use their language skills to construct narratives, an illustrated storytelling exercise is provided at the end of each lesson. These exercises require students to draw on what they have just learned in order to recount the story depicted.

Note: Prefaces to previous editions of IC are available at chengtsui.co.

中国的节日
中國的節日
China's Holidays

✓ Check off the following language functions as you learn how to:

[ ] Name major Chinese holidays, give their dates, and identify foods with which they are associated

[ ] Express Chinese New Year wishes

[ ] Describe Chinese New Year customs

[ ] Wish others success or good health

As you progress through the lesson, note other language functions you would like to learn.

_____

_____

_____

I. Listening Comprehension

A Listen to the Lesson Text audio, then circle the most appropriate choice. INTERPRETIVE

1 Why was the character 福 pasted upside down?

    a   It was put upside down by mistake.

    b   Xuemei's uncle and aunt grew up in the U.S. and can't read Chinese.

    c   The placement is based on a pun.

2 A Chinese New Year's Eve dinner should include fish because

    a   eating fish is good for one's health.

    b   fish are auspicious animals.

    c   the word for "fish" sounds like a different word that is auspicious.

3 What major traditional Chinese festivals besides Chinese New Year are mentioned in the dialogue?

    a   the Qingming and Dragon Boat Festivals

    b   the Dragon Boat and Mid-Autumn Festivals

    c   the Mid-Autumn and Qingming Festivals

4 What do Xuemei and Ke Lin receive from Xuemei's uncle and aunt as a New Year gift?

    a   cash

    b   a cellphone

    c   firecrackers

5 Who does Xuemei send Chinese New Year's greetings to after dinner?

    a   her parents and teachers

    b   her teachers and friends

    c   her parents and friends

B Listen to the Workbook Dialogue audio, then mark these statements true or false. INTERPRETIVE

1 ____ The speakers have lived in their current residence for less than a year.

2 ____ The dialogue most likely takes place at the dinner table.

3 ____ The man likes both their residence and their neighborhood.

4 ____ The woman thinks that they need more furniture.

5 ____ The speakers are happy that they don't have children.

6 ____ The speakers toast each other with tea.

C | Listen to the Workbook Narrative 1 audio, then mark these statements true or false. INTERPRETIVE

    1 ____   This voicemail is a Chinese New Year's greeting.

    2 ____   Little Jiang has been living in China for many years.

    3 ____   Little Jiang celebrated the Chinese New Year with his parents.

    4 ____   Little Jiang wants to hear about Little Lin's Chinese New Year's Eve dinner.

D | Listen to the Workbook Narrative 2 audio, then circle the most appropriate choice. INTERPRETIVE

    1   Where does Old Wang live?

        a   Sichuan

        b   Beijing

        c   elsewhere in China

    2   Why didn't Old Wang and Mrs. Wang make dinner reservations at a restaurant for New Year's Eve?

        a   All the good restaurants in town were completely booked.

        b   Their children prefer to eat at home.

        c   Mrs. Wang wanted to cook for her family.

    3   Why didn't their son light any firecrackers?

        a   They didn't buy any firecrackers.

        b   They didn't want to disturb others watching TV.

        c   They wanted to go to bed.

E | ____   Listen to the Workbook Listening Rejoinder audio. After hearing the first speaker, select the best response from the four choices given by the second speaker. Indicate the letter of your choice. INTERPRETIVE

II. Pinyin and Tone

A | Compare the pronunciations of the underlined characters in the two words or phrases given. Provide their initials in *pinyin*.

小区/小區 _____   初五 _____

B | Compare the tones of the underlined characters in the two words or phrases given. Indicate the tones with 1 (first tone), 2 (second tone), 3 (third tone), 4 (fourth tone), or 0 (neutral tone).

正月 _____   正好 _____

A Practice asking and answering these questions. INTERPERSONAL

1 你住的地方是租的还是买的？

　你住的地方是租的還是買的？

2 几房几厅几卫？

　幾房幾廳幾衛？

3 环境怎么样？住起来舒服不舒服？

　環境怎麼樣？住起來舒服不舒服？

4 除夕是哪一天？

5 今年过什么节你会回家跟家人团圆？

　今年過什麼節你會回家跟家人團圓？

B Practice speaking with these prompts. PRESENTATIONAL

1 请谈谈中国人怎么过春节。

　請談談中國人怎麼過春節。

2 请谈谈在你们的国家，人们怎么过新年。

　請談談在你們的國家，人們怎麼過新年。

3 Review the lesson and name the major traditional Chinese festivals, their dates, and the foods they are typically associated with. Which Chinese holiday appeals to you most? Why?

IV. Reading Comprehension

A Write the characters, *pinyin*, and English equivalent of each new word formed. Guess the meaning, then use a dictionary to confirm.

1 "社会"的"社" + "小区"的"区"

　"社會"的"社" + "小區"的"區"

　→ 社 + 区/區 → ＿＿＿＿＿＿ ＿＿＿＿＿＿

2 "幸福"的"福" + "天气"的"气"

　"幸福"的"福" + "天氣"的"氣"

　→ 福 + 气/氣 → ＿＿＿＿＿＿ ＿＿＿＿＿＿ ＿＿＿＿＿＿

3 "奇怪"的"怪" + "购物"的"物"

　"奇怪"的"怪" + "購物"的"物"

　→ 怪 + 物 → ＿＿＿＿＿＿ ＿＿＿＿＿＿

4 "月饼"的"饼" + "干杯"的"干"

　"月餅"的"餅" + "乾杯"的"乾"

　→ 饼/餅 + 干/乾 → ＿＿＿＿＿＿ ＿＿＿＿＿＿ ＿＿＿＿＿＿

5 "拜年"的"年" + "蛋糕"的"糕"

　→ 年 + 糕 → ＿＿＿＿＿＿ ＿＿＿＿＿＿ ＿＿＿＿＿＿

B Read the dialogue, then fill in the blanks with the phrases provided. INTERPRETIVE

住起来　　吃起来　　穿起来　　喝起来　　做起来

Person A: 您的新家环境真不错，＿＿＿＿＿＿很舒服吧?

Person B: 还行，挺安静的。请喝咖啡。

Person A: 谢谢! ……您这咖啡＿＿＿＿＿＿特别香。您得告诉我您在咖啡里边放了什么。

Person B: 咖啡里什么都没放，＿＿＿＿＿＿很简单，有空我教你。来，吃点儿月饼。

Person A:	您的月饼 _____ 真香，肯定很贵吧？
Person B:	我也不清楚，是朋友送的。我今天穿的这件衣服，也是同一个朋友送的。
Person A:	您的朋友真会买东西。这件衣服，您 _____ 特别好看。

住起來　　吃起來　　穿起來　　喝起來　　做起來

Person A:	您的新家環境真不錯，_____ 很舒服吧？
Person B:	還行，挺安靜的。請喝咖啡。
Person A:	謝謝！⋯⋯您這咖啡 _____ 特別香。您得告訴我您在咖啡裡邊放了什麼。
Person B:	咖啡裡什麼都沒放，_____ 很簡單，有空我教你。來，吃點兒月餅。
Person A:	您的月餅 _____ 真香，肯定很貴吧？
Person B:	我也不清楚，是朋友送的。我今天穿的這件衣服，也是同一個朋友送的。
Person A:	您的朋友真會買東西。這件衣服，您 _____ 特別好看。

C Read this passage, then mark the statements true or false. INTERPRETIVE

　　雪梅已经两年没有和爸爸妈妈一起过春节了。这次回杭州，她原来打算陪父母过完年以后再去北京，可是舅舅从北京打电话说有一个实习的机会，马上就要开始工作。爸爸妈妈也说，这个机会对雪梅的事业太重要了，就让雪梅和柯林春节前去了北京。雪梅在北京给妈妈打电话说，她和柯林已经在杭州一家有名的餐馆儿给爸爸妈妈和弟弟订好了去那儿吃年夜饭，这样妈妈就不用花时间准备了。可是妈妈说，到餐馆儿吃方便是方便，可是没有在家里吃年夜饭好。雪梅觉得妈妈说的有道理，就打电话告诉那家餐馆儿说不去了。

雪梅已經兩年沒有和爸爸媽媽一起過春節了。這次回杭州，她原來打算陪父母過完年以後再去北京，可是舅舅從北京打電話說有一個實習的機會，馬上就要開始工作。爸爸媽媽也說，這個機會對雪梅的事業太重要了，就讓雪梅和柯林春節前去了北京。雪梅在北京給媽媽打電話說，她和柯林已經在杭州一家有名的餐館兒給爸爸媽媽和弟弟訂好了去那兒吃年夜飯，這樣媽媽就不用花時間準備了。可是媽媽說，到餐館兒吃方便是方便，可是沒有在家裡吃年夜飯好。雪梅覺得媽媽說的有道理，就打電話告訴那家餐館兒說不去了。

1 ___ Xuemei went to Beijing earlier than she had originally planned.

2 ___ Xuemei feels bad that she has spent only one Spring Festival with her parents in the last two years.

3 ___ Xuemei had intended to cook a New Year's Eve dinner for her family.

4 ___ Xuemei's parents and brother will most likely have their New Year's Eve dinner at home.

5 ___ Xuemei's parents persuaded Xuemei to leave for Beijing before the Spring Festival because they thought that Xuemei's uncle would need her company in Beijing.

D Read this passage, then mark the statements true or false. INTERPRETIVE

　　在中国，很多人在过春节的时候都说吉利 (jílì) (auspicious) 的话，可是有时候说吉利的话不太容易。有一位王先生，家里的家具都很新很漂亮，他觉得过年应该在墙上贴两张画才像过年。他贴好了第一张，想把第二张贴得跟第一张一样高，就对十岁的儿子说："你帮我看看，要是我把画贴得太高了，你就说'发财'；要是太低了，你就说'健康'。"说着，王先生就把第二张画贴到墙上了，贴得正好，不比第一张高，也不比第一张低。这时候儿子高兴地说："爸爸，你太棒了，不发财，也不健康！"

　　在中國，很多人在過春節的時候都說吉利 (jílì) (auspicious) 的話，可是有時候說吉利的話不太容易。有一位王先生，家裡的傢俱都很新很漂亮，他覺得過年應該在牆上貼兩張畫才像過年。他貼好了第一張，想把第二張貼得跟第一張一樣高，就對十歲的兒子說："你幫我看看，要是我把畫貼得太高了，你就說'發財'；要是太低了，你就說'健康'。"說著，王先生就把第二張畫貼到牆上了，貼得正好，不比第一張高，也不比第一張低。這時候兒子高興地說："爸爸，你太棒了，不發財，也不健康！"

1 ____ According to the passage, saying the right auspicious thing is not always easy.

2 ____ Mr. Wang thinks that pasting a couple of pictures on the wall will enhance the festive atmosphere.

3 ____ Of Mr. Wang's two pictures, the first has to do with wealth and the second has to do with health.

4 ____ Mr. Wang tries to get his son to say auspicious words.

5 ____ Mr. Wang's son is glad that his father was able to position the pictures perfectly.

6 ____ Mr. Wang's son knows that his father will be neither wealthy nor healthy.

E Look at the apartment listing below and note in English the things that you like and dislike about the place. Before calling the landlord, jot down in Chinese some of the questions you may want to ask. Note: 二居室 has the same meaning as 两个卧室/兩個臥室.

INTERPRETIVE & PRESENTATIONAL

出租二居室

出租本小区二居室，室内非常干净，环境好，有电视、冰箱、双人床、写字桌。没有空调、洗衣机。希望你爱干净，如果你有意租房，就给我打电话吧。

联系人：徐先生 137182XXXXX

出租二居室

出租本小區二居室，室內非常乾淨，環境好，有電視、冰箱、雙人床、寫字桌。沒有空調、洗衣機。希望你愛乾淨，如果你有意租房，就給我打電話吧。

聯繫人：徐先生 137182XXXXX

Likes: _____

Dislikes: _____

Questions: _____

A Form a character by combining the given components as indicated. Then use that character to write a word, phrase, or short sentence.

1   左边一个人字旁，右边一个"到"，

   左邊一個人字旁，右邊一個"到"，

   是 _____ 的 ____。

2   左边一个"工作"的"工"，右边一个"力气"的"力"，

   左邊一個"工作"的"工"，右邊一個"力氣"的"力"，

   是 _____ 的 ____。

3   左边一个三点水，右边一个"良好"的"良"，

   左邊一個三點水，右邊一個"良好"的"良"，

   是 _____ 的 ____。

4   左边一个人字旁，右边一个"专业"的"专"，

   左邊一個人字旁，右邊一個"專業"的"專"，

   是 _____ 的 ____。

5   外边一个"口"，里边一个"售货员"的"员"，

   外邊一個"口"，裡邊一個"售貨員"的"員"，

   是 _____ 的 ____。

6   左边一个"贝"，右边一个"刚才"的"才"，

   左邊一個"貝"，右邊一個"剛才"的"才"，

   是 _____ 的 ____。

7   上边一个"因为"的"因"，下边一个"心事"的"心"，

   上邊一個"因為"的"因"，下邊一個"心事"的"心"，

   是 _____ 的 ____。

Person A: 天明忙着做什么呢？
天明忙著做什麼呢？

Person B: 他忙着打扫房间呢。
他忙著打掃房間呢。

1

_____

_____

2

_____

_____

3

_____

_____

C Summarize the IC characters' routines using 先⋯再⋯, following the example below.

PRESENTATIONAL

having soup 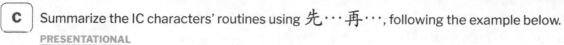 having (other) food

张天明一般都先喝汤再吃饭。
張天明一般都先喝湯再吃飯。

1

doing homework having dinner

_____

2

working at the library swimming at the athletic center

_____

3

taking a shower having breakfast

_____

出租一居

One-bedroom apartment for rent. Close to BLCU and ten-minute walk from subway. TV, fridge, washing machine, air-conditioner, microwave, bed, desk, table, sofa, tea table, and so on... Internet and hot water 24 hours.

Telephone number: 158016XXXXX Joe

_____

E Translate these dialogues into Chinese. PRESENTATIONAL

1 Q: What have you decided to do after the semester ends?

_____

A: Go to New York to intern and find a job.

_____

2 Q: Where you're from (你们那儿/你們那兒), can you set off firecrackers for the Spring Festival?

_____

A: No. We can't buy firecrackers, either.

_____

3 Q: What Thanksgiving traditions does your family have?

_____

A: My family eats together on Thanksgiving. After lunch we watch American football. It's very lively in my house on Thanksgiving.

_____

_____

4　Q:　How is the environment of your residential development?

_____

A:　The environment is very nice, very quiet. And it's very close to school, really convenient.

_____

5　Q:　Where did you go for the Spring Festival?

_____

A:　I went to Hangzhou to see my (maternal) uncle and aunt. They have a three-bedroom, one-dining room, one-living room, two-bathroom apartment. It's very comfortable [to live there].

_____

_____

Q:　When did you get to Hangzhou?

_____

A:　I got to Hangzhou on New Year's Eve. My uncle and aunt took me to a restaurant, so we didn't have New Year's Eve dinner at their home.

_____

Q:　Do your uncle and his wife cook?

_____

A:　They really like cooking, but they are very busy with work. They often don't have time to cook.

_____

Q:　What do your uncle and aunt do?

_____

A:　My uncle is a university professor. My aunt is a lawyer.

_____

6 **Person A:** My Chinese classmate invited me to have dinner on Chinese New Year's Eve at her house. I wonder (I don't know) what Chinese people have for dinner on Chinese New Year's Eve.

_____

_____

Person B: If your classmate's family is from the North, they'll definitely have dumplings.

_____

Person A: Great! I like eating dumplings. What else?

_____

Person B: Chinese people must also have fish at dinner on Chinese New Year's Eve. Furthermore, you can't eat it all. You have to leave some on the plate.

_____

_____

Person A: Why? Isn't that wasteful?

_____

Person B: Because "fish" is pronounced the same as "surplus," in other words, "leaving some behind."

_____

Person A: How interesting! Thank you for telling me. Otherwise, I'd probably eat the whole fish.

_____

_____

F Translate this passage into Chinese. PRESENTATIONAL

China has many traditional holidays. Besides the Spring Festival, there are also the Lantern Festival, the Dragon Boat Festival, the Mid-Autumn Festival, and the Qingming Festival (清明节/清明節). Every year, the fifteenth day of the first month on the lunar calendar is the Lantern Festival. On that day, Chinese people eat *yuanxiao*. April 5 is the Qingming Festival, which is also an important traditional holiday. The fifth day of the fifth month of the lunar calendar is the Dragon Boat Festival. Every Chinese family eats *zongzi*. The fifteenth day of the eighth month of the lunar calendar is the Mid-Autumn Festival, which is a day of family reunion—a bit like America's Thanksgiving. Everyone eats moon cakes to celebrate the Mid-Autumn Festival.

_____

_____

_____

_____

_____

_____

G It's that time of year again—time to call, text message, email, or write a card to your Chinese friends and their families to wish them a happy Chinese New Year. Make sure your New Year wishes are appropriate given your relationship with the recipient. Fill in the table, indicating who you will contact, how you will contact them, and what you will say or write. PRESENTATIONAL

Name	Mode of Communication	Wishes
Person 1: 老师/老師	写卡片/寫卡片	
Person 2:		
Person 3:		
Person 4:		
Person 5:		
Person 6:		

From among your friends and relatives, choose one to call. Rehearse your message with a partner or record a message for your teacher. Choose another person to write a letter or an email to. Write down your message to that person:

_____

_____

_____

_____

H Find two or three photos of a Chinese holiday by searching online or asking friends and family. Write a brief news article or a letter to a friend in Chinese describing the pictures. Make sure to describe the atmosphere, what people are doing and eating, how the places are decorated, etc. You can use your imagination to make up quotes from people celebrating the festival. Use at least two of the grammar patterns and five new words and phrases from this lesson. PRESENTATIONAL

I This year, you will be starting a new tradition by hosting a Chinese New Year celebration for your family. Write an email to your family members describing how they can help decorate and cook for the holiday, what they should expect to do, what they should wear, what they should bring, etc. The more details you provide about the celebration, the more fun it will be! Use at least three of the grammar patterns or words and phrases from this lesson. PRESENTATIONAL

J Write a story in Chinese based on the four images below. Make sure that your story has a beginning, middle, and end, and that the transition from one picture to the next is smooth and logical. PRESENTATIONAL

_____

_____

_____

_____

_____

中国的变化
中國的變化
Changes in China

✓ Check off the following language functions as you learn how to:

〔 〕 Describe ways in which a place has or hasn't changed

〔 〕 Indicate that something is different from what you expected

〔 〕 Express concern about the consequences of a persistent state

〔 〕 Compare a place with what it used to be like

As you progress through the lesson, note other language functions you would like to learn.

_____

_____

_____

A Listen to the Lesson Text audio, then mark these statements true or false. INTERPRETIVE

1 ____ Tianming and Lisha will return to the United States right after visiting Nanjing.

2 ____ Nanjing is not like what Lisha had expected.

3 ____ Like his visitors, Tianming's cousin is concerned that Nanjing does not look distinctly Chinese.

4 ____ Tianming fails to find his father's middle school in Nanjing.

5 ____ Tianming's cousin wants to show his visitors around more sights before breaking for lunch.

B Listen to the Workbook Dialogue audio, then mark these statements true or false. INTERPRETIVE

1 ____ Both speakers have been away from this place for some time.

2 ____ The speakers are in a very quiet environment.

3 ____ The restaurant has expanded its business in recent years.

4 ____ The parking lot in front of the restaurant is full of cars and bicycles.

5 ____ The restaurant's menu has not changed very much over the years.

6 ____ The customers of the restaurant nowadays like the same types of food that customers of the past preferred.

C Listen to the Workbook Narrative 1 audio, then mark these statements true or false. INTERPRETIVE

1 ____ Mr. Qian went to college in Beijing.

2 ____ Many of the places in Hangzhou familiar to Mr. Qian no longer exist.

3 ____ Mr. Qian is pleased with how much his hometown has changed.

D Listen to the Workbook Narrative 2 audio, then circle the most appropriate choice. INTERPRETIVE

1 How does the speaker describe old Nanjing?

   a It had few high-rises and many trees.

   b It had few high-rises but many cars.

   c It had many trees and many cars.

2 According to the speaker, what does Nanjing look like now?

   a It has many trees, many cars, and many high-rises.

   b It has few trees, many cars, and many high-rises.

   c It has many trees, many cars, and few high-rises.

3 On the street, the speaker hears people talking in

    a   Mandarin.

    b   Shanghai dialect.

    c   Nanjing dialect.

4 How does the speaker feel about the changes unfolding in Nanjing?

    a   happy

    b   concerned

    c   indifferent

E ____ Listen to the Workbook Listening Rejoinder audio. After hearing the first speaker, select the best response from the four choices given by the second speaker. Indicate the letter of your choice. INTERPRETIVE

II. Pinyin and Tone

A Compare the pronunciations of the underlined characters in the two words or phrases given. Provide their initials in *pinyin*.

一<u>句</u>话/一<u>句</u>話 _____   帮<u>助</u>/幫<u>助</u> _____

B Compare the tones of the underlined characters in the two words or phrases given. Indicate the tones with 1 (first tone), 2 (second tone), 3 (third tone), 4 (fourth tone), or 0 (neutral tone).

<u>导</u>游/<u>導</u>遊 _____   <u>道</u>歉 _____

III. Speaking

A Practice asking and answering these questions. INTERPERSONAL

1 你坐过高铁吗？坐过几次？从哪儿坐到哪儿？

你坐過高鐵嗎？坐過幾次？從哪兒坐到哪兒？

2 你喜欢住在安静的城市还是热闹的城市？为什么？

你喜歡住在安靜的城市還是熱鬧的城市？為什麼？

3 你们的城市新盖的高楼多还是传统的建筑多？你喜欢住
在新盖的高楼里还是传统的建筑里？为什么？

你們的城市新蓋的高樓多還是傳統的建築多？你喜歡住
在新蓋的高樓裡還是傳統的建築裡？為什麼？

4 你游览过哪些城市？对哪个城市的印象最好？为什么？

你遊覽過哪些城市？對哪個城市的印象最好？為什麼？

B Practice speaking with these prompts. PRESENTATIONAL

1 请谈谈你的家乡有什么特色。

請談談你的家鄉有什麼特色。

2 请谈谈你的家乡最近几年有些什么变化。

請談談你的家鄉最近幾年有些什麼變化。

3 Review the lesson. In Chinese, share your answers to these questions with your class: Do you prefer places with traditional characteristics or modern excitement? Do you enjoy visiting cities with popular tourist sights, or those with convenient shopping centers?

IV. Reading Comprehension

A Write the characters, *pinyin*, and English equivalent of each new word formed. Guess the meaning, then use a dictionary to confirm.

1 "绿色"的"绿" + "变化"的"化"

"綠色"的"綠" + "變化"的"化"

→ 绿/綠 + 化 → _____ _____ _____

2 "上班"的"班" + "公共汽车"的"车"

"上班"的"班" + "公共汽車"的"車"

→ 班/班 + 车/車 → _____ _____ _____

3 "一座山"的"座" + "位子"的"位"

→ 座 + 位 → _____ _____ _____

4 "回来"的"回" + "声音"的"声"

　"回來"的"回" + "聲音"的"聲"

　→ 回 + 声/聲 → ＿＿＿＿＿＿　＿＿＿＿＿＿　＿＿＿＿＿＿

5 "农村"的"农" + "民以食为天"的"民"

　"農村"的"農" + "民以食為天"的"民"

　→ 农/農 + 民 → ＿＿＿＿＿＿　＿＿＿＿＿＿　＿＿＿＿＿＿

B Read the dialogue, then fill in the blanks with the phrases provided. INTERPRETIVE

　尽可能　　看起来　　怎么　　从来　　非…不可

Person A: 元宵节快到了，我们做点元宵吃，怎么样？

Person B: 做元宵？我不行，＿＿＿＿＿＿ 没做过。

Person A: 你在中国出生、长大的，＿＿＿＿＿＿ 没做过元宵？

Person B: 我最不喜欢进厨房，能不做菜就＿＿＿＿＿＿ 不做菜。别说做元宵了，我连一般的菜都不太会。

Person A: ＿＿＿＿＿＿ 这次做元宵得靠我了。

Person B: 没错，＿＿＿＿＿＿ 得靠你＿＿＿＿＿＿ 。

　儘可能　　看起來　　怎麼　　從來　　非…不可

Person A: 元宵節快到了，我們做點元宵吃，怎麼樣？

Person B: 做元宵？我不行，＿＿＿＿＿＿ 沒做過。

Person A: 你在中國出生、長大的，＿＿＿＿＿＿ 沒做過元宵？

Person B: 我最不喜歡進廚房，能不做菜就＿＿＿＿＿＿ 不做菜。別說做元宵了，我連一般的菜都不太會。

Person A: ＿＿＿＿＿＿ 這次做元宵得靠我了。

Person B: 沒錯，＿＿＿＿＿＿ 得靠你＿＿＿＿＿＿ 。

Complete each dialogue by selecting the most appropriate response from the choices provided. Indicate the letter of your choice. INTERPRETIVE

a 别着急，我们尽可能帮你找。

别著急，我們儘可能幫你找。

b 出去旅行应该尽可能少带东西。

出去旅行應該儘可能少帶東西。

c 请尽可能早点来。

請儘可能早點來。

d 我们应该尽可能保留有特点的传统建筑。

我們應該儘可能保留有特點的傳統建築。

1 Person A: 请问，我明天什么时候来上班？

請問，我明天什麼時候來上班？

Person B: _____

2 Person A: 糟糕，我的电脑丢了。

糟糕，我的電腦丟了。

Person B: _____

3 Person A: 等等我，我行李还没有准备好。

等等我，我行李還沒有準備好。

Person B: _____

4 Person A: 我们怎么让更多的游客来我们这儿旅游呢？

我們怎麼讓更多的遊客來我們這兒旅遊呢？

Person B: _____

Read the passage, then mark the statements true or false. INTERPRETIVE

如果你没去过城南的"小吃一条街"，你一定得去看看。那儿有很多餐馆，湖南的、四川的、上海的、广东的，都是传统建筑。一到晚上，小吃街上和建筑上的灯都亮了，五颜六色，非常漂亮。七点左右，街上就都是人，还有不少老外呢。你别以为他们是来看那些传统建筑的，他们是来尝尝餐馆里的传统小吃的。有的餐馆里人太多，你得等半个多小时才能买到一份小吃。虽然我们这个城市现在有不少美国快餐店，可是去"小吃一条街"的人还是很多。不管是"老中"还是"老外"，大家都喜欢中国的传统小吃。二十年来，这个城市完全变了，只有"小吃一条街"保留了自己的特色。

如果你沒去過城南的"小吃一條街"，你一定得去看看。那兒有很多餐館，湖南的、四川的、上海的、廣東的，都是傳統建築。一到晚上，小吃街上和建築上的燈都亮了，五顏六色，非常漂亮。七點左右，街上就都是人，還有不少老外呢。你別以為他們是來看那些傳統建築的，他們是來嚐嚐餐館裡的傳統小吃的。有的餐館裡人太多，你得等半個多小時才能買到一份小吃。雖然我們這個城市現在有不少美國快餐店，可是去"小吃一條街"的人還是很多。不管是"老中"還是"老外"，大家都喜歡中國的傳統小吃。二十年來，這個城市完全變了，只有"小吃一條街"保留了自己的特色。

1 ____ The street described in the passage is in the northern part of the city.

2 ____ Along the street, there are Chinese restaurants serving different styles of cooking.

3 ____ In the evening, the street is full of people admiring the architecture.

4 ____ Some of the restaurants are over half an hour away.

5 ____ In this city, traditional Chinese snacks remain popular despite the increasing number of American fast food restaurants.

E Based on the passage in (D), circle the most appropriate choice. INTERPRETIVE

1   Which of these statements about the street described in the passage is most accurate?

a   It is the only place in the city that offers traditional Chinese food.

b   It is the only place in the city that has remained largely unchanged over the last two decades.

c   It is the only place in the city where there isn't an American fast food restaurant.

2   Who are the intended readers of this passage?

a   restaurant owners

b   architects

c   visitors to the city

F Read the passage, then mark the statements true or false. INTERPRETIVE

广生，

　　看到你昨天的电子邮件，知道你计划今年暑假回广州，我太高兴了，真希望暑假明天就开始。我特别高兴的是，你没忘记我们以前常去的新元电影院。我和你一样，也很希望我们能一起再去那儿看一次电影。可是我得告诉你，新元电影院那里半年前盖了一个新的地铁站。你知道我们这儿以前是一个很安静的地方，可是有了地铁以后，就变得热闹了。还记得新元电影院对面的那两家小鞋店吗？那儿现在成了一家日本银行和一家美国快餐店了。你在法国的这两年，广州的变化真的是太大了。虽然广州变化那么大，可是我没变，我还是两年前的我。

爱你的，
小花

廣生，

　　看到你昨天的電子郵件，知道你計劃今年暑假回廣州，我太高興了，真希望暑假明天就開始。我特別高興的是，你沒忘記我們以前常去的新元電影院。我和你一樣，也很希望我們能一起再去那兒看一次電影。可是我得告訴你，新元電影院那裡半年前蓋了一個新的地鐵站。你知道我們這兒以前是一個很安靜的地方，可是有了地鐵以後，就變得熱鬧了。還記得新元電影院對面的那兩家小鞋店嗎？那兒現在成了一家日本銀行和一家美國快餐店了。你在法國的這兩年，廣州的變化真的是太大了。雖然廣州變化那麼大，可是我沒變，我還是兩年前的我。

愛你的，
小花

1 ____ Guangsheng left Guangzhou for France two years ago.

2 ____ This email was most likely written in October.

3 ____ When Guangsheng was in Guangzhou, he lived close to a subway station.

4 ____ When Guangsheng is back in Guangzhou, Xiaohua will see a movie with him at the movie theater that they used to go to.

G Based on the passage in (F), circle the most appropriate choice. INTERPRETIVE

1 Which of the following places did Guangsheng most likely mention in his initial email to Xiaohua?

a the movie theater

b the subway station

c shoe stores

2 What does the final sentence of Xiaohua's email suggest?

a Even though Guangzhou has changed a lot, Guangsheng will not get lost in the city.

b Despite the changes in their neighborhood, Guangzhou remains largely the same.

c Her feelings for Guangsheng haven't changed.

3 What is the most likely relationship between Guangsheng and Xiaohua?

a teacher and student

b boyfriend and girlfriend

c casual acquaintances

H Look at this store sign and answer the questions in English. INTERPRETIVE

1 张天明从来没去过这个城市，你呢？

张天明從來沒去過這個城市，你呢？

_____

2 他们卖的东西里，你认识哪些？请你选一、两个翻译成
英文。

他們賣的東西裡，你認識哪些？請你選一、兩個翻譯成
英文。

_____

I Look at this restaurant's slogan and answer the question. INTERPRETIVE

你已经学过第一句话了，你觉得第二句话的意思是什么
呢？请翻译成英文。

你已經學過第一句話了，你覺得第二句話的意思是什麼
呢？請翻譯成英文。

_____

A Form a character by combining the given components as indicated. Then use that character to write a word, phrase, or short sentence.

1　外边一个"银行"的"行"，中间上、下两个"土"，

　　外邊一個"銀行"的"行"，中間上、下兩個"土"，

　　是 ＿＿＿＿＿＿ 的 ＿＿＿＿ 。

2　左边一个"马"，右边一个"奇怪"的"奇"，

　　左邊一個"馬"，右邊一個"奇怪"的"奇"，

　　是 ＿＿＿＿＿＿ 的 ＿＿＿＿ 。

3　左边一个"女"，右边一个"生"，

　　左邊一個"女"，右邊一個"生"，

　　是 ＿＿＿＿＿＿ 的 ＿＿＿＿ 。

4　外边一个"广"，里边一个"坐"，

　　外邊一個"广"，裡邊一個"坐"，

　　是 ＿＿＿＿＿＿ 的 ＿＿＿＿ 。

5　左边一个"口"，右边一个"合适"的"合"，

　　左邊一個"口"，右邊一個"合適"的"合"，

　　是 ＿＿＿＿＿＿ 的 ＿＿＿＿ 。

要不是出租汽车师傅帮忙，张天明是不可能找回他的
电脑的。

要不是出租汽車師傅幫忙，張天明是不可能找回他的
電腦的。

1

_____ ，

柯林上课非迟到不可。

柯林上課非遲到不可。

2

自助西餐
幸福超市
皮件皮包
咖啡
大酒店
旅行社

_____ ，

丽莎还以为她在纽约呢。

麗莎還以為她在紐約呢。

3

_____,
柯林吃年夜饭的时候就会把鱼都吃了。
柯林吃年夜飯的時候就會把魚都吃了。

C Based on the images, complete the statements using 从来/從來, following the example below.
PRESENTATIONAL

林雪梅的妈妈从来不喝咖啡。
林雪梅的媽媽從來不喝咖啡。

1

Menu
$$$$
$$$$

我从来不_____。
我從來不_____。

2

名牌

我姐姐从来不_____。
我姐姐從來不_____。

3 日本

我从来没_____。
我從來沒_____。

4

我弟弟从来不＿＿＿＿＿＿＿＿＿＿＿＿＿＿＿。

我弟弟從來不＿＿＿＿＿＿＿＿＿＿＿＿＿＿＿。

D Based on the images, use 看起来／看起來 to complete the dialogues. INTERPERSONAL

1 Q: 他今天晚上会来吗？

他今天晚上會來嗎？

A: ＿＿＿＿＿＿＿＿＿＿＿＿＿＿＿＿＿＿＿。

2 Q: 柯林喜欢吃月饼吗？

柯林喜歡吃月餅嗎？

A: ＿＿＿＿＿＿＿＿＿＿＿＿＿＿＿＿＿＿＿。

3 Q: 雪梅会滑冰吗？

雪梅會滑冰嗎？

A: ＿＿＿＿＿＿＿＿＿＿＿＿＿＿＿＿＿＿＿。

4 Q: 雪梅舅舅、舅妈两个人幸福不幸福？

雪梅舅舅、舅媽兩個人幸福不幸福？

A: ＿＿＿＿＿＿＿＿＿＿＿＿＿＿＿＿＿＿＿。

Translate these dialogues into Chinese. PRESENTATIONAL

1 Q: Cousin (表哥), we've arrived at the train station. Where are you?

_____

   A: I'm almost there. Sorry, the roads are jammed. Wait for me. Don't go running around.

_____

   Q: Where should we wait for you, then?

_____

   A: When you come out of the train station, there's a shopping center next to it. Wait for me at the entrance to the shopping center.

_____

_____

2 Person A: What's that sound?

_____

   Person B: Sorry, it's my stomach rumbling. I'm hungry.

_____

   Person A: What would you like to eat? There are many shops selling local snacks across the street.

_____

   Person B: Do you want to have *zongzi*?

_____

   Person A: Since it's the Lantern Festival today, let's have *yuanxiao*.

_____

F | Translate these passages into Chinese. PRESENTATIONAL

1 Lisha's Diary

Today Tianming's cousin acted as our tour guide and took us to walk around the streets and see a bit of Nanjing. Tianming's father often says that Nanjing is a quiet city. Who knew it would be this lively and bustling with activity? There are foreign tourists everywhere. There are American fast food restaurants, Japanese banks, and French clothing stores in Nanjing. Tianming said that Nanjing has melded into the world, which is a good thing. But I worry that if things go on like this, there could be fewer and fewer things with Chinese characteristics. Tianming's cousin said that Nanjing has preserved many things with Chinese characteristics, for example, the Temple of Confucius. When we saw the Temple of Confucius, we all felt it was really interesting. It seems that people in Nanjing do really want to preserve the traditions of old Nanjing as much as possible.

_____

_____

_____

_____

_____

_____

_____

_____

_____

2   OK. We've arrived at the Temple of Confucius. I'll give a short introduction to the history of the Temple of Confucius. Nanjing's Temple of Confucius was first (最早) built in 1034, so it has a history of almost one thousand years. The architecture that we can see now isn't as old as that, but it is very characteristic of old Nanjing. We can all see that there are many Chinese and foreign tourists here. So who was Confucius? He was a very famous philosopher. In the past, many places in China had a Temple of Confucius. Many people would go to the Temple of Confucius to pay their respects to Confucius (拜孔子), hoping that they would do well on exams.

_____

_____

_____

_____

_____

_____

_____

G   Choose a city or another place with a long history, and write a paragraph in Chinese offering your suggestions for promoting tourism there. Use at least two grammar patterns and five words or phrases from this lesson. PRESENTATIONAL

H Write a story in Chinese based on the four images below. Make sure that your story has a beginning, middle, and end, and that the transition from one picture to the next is smooth and logical. PRESENTATIONAL

_____

_____

_____

_____

_____

_____

_____

_____

去云南旅游
去雲南旅遊
A Trip to Yunnan

 Check off the following language functions as you learn how to:

[ ] Describe what costs a package tour may cover

[ ] Explain the difference between "soft" and "hard" sleeper cars

[ ] Describe Yunnan's natural and cultural attractions

[ ] Discuss high and low points of a trip

As you progress through the lesson, note other language functions you would like to learn.

_____

_____

_____

I. Listening Comprehension

A Listen to the Lesson Text audio, then mark these statements true or false. INTERPRETIVE

1 ____ Zhang Tianming opted for a hard sleeper berth so that he could practice speaking Chinese with other passengers.

2 ____ Zhang Tianming liked the food in the dining car.

3 ____ Zhang Tianming and Lisha arrived in Kunming more than two hours earlier than their friends.

B Listen to the Lesson Text audio, then circle the most appropriate choice. INTERPRETIVE

1 The Stone Forest consists of

  a trees among rocks.

  b trees that look like rocks.

  c rocks that look like trees.

2 Who enjoyed shopping for souvenirs?

  a Xuemei and Lisha

  b Ke Lin and Tianming

  c Ke Lin and Lisha

3 When Zhang Tianming and his friends spent the evening in Lijiang, what did they do before returning to the hotel?

  a shopped for souvenirs

  b drank tea at a teahouse

  c walked along the river

C Listen to the Workbook Dialogue audio, then mark these statements true or false. INTERPRETIVE

1 ____ The man and the woman recently went to Lijiang together.

2 ____ If the woman had wanted to save time, she could have eaten meals at her hotel.

3 ____ The woman didn't like the souvenir stores in her hotel.

4 ____ The woman didn't look for a family-run bed-and-breakfast because she thought it would be more expensive.

5 ____ According to the man, staying at a bed-and-breakfast provides more opportunities to engage with the local customs and culture.

6 ____ According to the man, only big hotels in Lijiang would provide free Internet access.

7 ____ If the woman had had this conversation before her trip, she would have stayed at a different place in Lijiang.

D Listen to the Workbook Narrative 1 audio, then circle the most appropriate choice. INTERPRETIVE

1 The speaker traveled from
   a Beijing to Guangzhou.
   b Guangzhou to Hangzhou.
   c Hangzhou to Guangzhou.

2 The speaker bought a ticket for the soft sleeper berth because he thought it would be
   a clean and quiet.
   b clean and spacious.
   c spacious and quiet.

3 The speaker didn't have a good night's sleep because a fellow passenger
   a talked on the phone all night.
   b made a lot of noise all night.
   c chatted with him all night.

E Listen to the Workbook Narrative 2 audio, then circle the most appropriate choice. INTERPRETIVE

1 Why does the speaker leave this message?
   a The recipient wants to travel with her.
   b The recipient wants to travel with Little Qian.
   c The recipient wants to travel to a city she had visited with Little Qian.

2 What was included in the price for the group tour?
   a plane tickets, meals, hotel rooms, and entrance tickets to tourist attractions
   b hotel rooms, meals, train tickets, and entrance tickets to tourist attractions
   c hotel rooms, bus tours, meals, and entrance tickets to tourist attractions

3 According to the speaker, what was the worst part of the group tour?
   a the shopping stops
   b the meals
   c the hotel

4 The speaker suggests that the recipient should join a group tour that
   a does not go to Harbin.
   b does not include shopping.
   c does not include meals.

F ____ Listen to the Workbook Listening Rejoinder audio. After hearing the first speaker, select the best response from the four choices given by the second speaker. Indicate the letter of your choice. INTERPRETIVE

A Compare the pronunciations of the underlined characters in the two words or phrases given. Provide their finals in *pinyin*.

旅<u>游</u>/旅<u>遊</u> _____   路<u>线</u>/路<u>線</u> _____

B Compare the tones of the underlined characters in the two words or phrases given. Indicate the tones with 1 (first tone), 2 (second tone), 3 (third tone), 4 (fourth tone), or 0 (neutral tone).

车<u>厢</u>/車<u>廂</u> _____   想<u>像</u>/想<u>像</u> _____

III. Speaking

A Practice asking and answering these questions. INTERPERSONAL

1 你喜欢参加旅行团还是自己去旅游？

你喜歡參加旅行團還是自己去旅遊？

2 对你来说，参加旅行团时，什么最重要？

對你來說，參加旅行團時，什麼最重要？

3 你觉得旅行团的团费应该包括什么？

你覺得旅行團的團費應該包括什麼？

B Practice speaking with these prompts. PRESENTATIONAL

1 请谈谈如果你在中国坐火车旅行，你会买硬卧还是买软卧的车票。为什么？

請談談如果你在中國坐火車旅行，你會買硬臥還是買軟臥的車票。為什麼？

2 请谈谈看了课文后，你想不想去云南旅游？为什么？

请談談看了課文後，你想不想去雲南旅遊？為什麼？

3 Describe your ideal vacation, including destinations (historic sites, natural scenic areas, etc.), time of year, means of transportation, and whether you would join a tour group or travel independently.

IV. Reading Comprehension

A Write the characters, *pinyin*, and English equivalent of each new word formed. Guess the meaning, then use a dictionary to confirm.

1 "分享"的"享" + "受到"的"受"

→ 享 + 受 → _____ _____ _____

2 "硬卧"的"硬" + "软件"的"件"

"硬臥"的"硬" + "軟件"的"件"

→ 硬 + 件 → _____ _____ _____

3 "起床"的"床" + "卧铺"的"铺"

"起床"的"床" + "臥鋪"的"鋪"

→ 床 + 铺/鋪 → _____ _____ _____

4 "包括"的"包" + "车厢"的"厢"

"包括"的"包" + "車廂"的"廂"

→ 包 + 厢/廂 → _____ _____ _____

5 "方便面"的"面" + "一条河"的"条"

"方便麵"的"麵" + "一條河"的"條"

→ 面/麵 + 条/條 → _____ _____ _____

B Fill in the blanks with the phrases provided. INTERPRETIVE

五颜六色的/五顏六色的   千奇百怪的

一干二净的/一乾二淨的   丢三拉四的

乱七八糟的/亂七八糟的

1 张天明很马虎，常常 _____。

   張天明很馬虎，常常 _____。

2 张天明的房间常常是 _____。

   張天明的房間常常是 _____。

3 柯林每顿饭都吃得 _____。

   柯林每頓飯都吃得 _____。

4 夫子庙附近很热闹，卖的东西 _____。

   夫子廟附近很熱鬧，賣的東西 _____。

5 石林石头的样子 _____。

   石林石頭的樣子 _____。

C Read this passage, then mark the statements true or false. INTERPRETIVE

    我认识大理的一位陈先生，他和太太开家庭旅馆。大理附近的旅游景点很多，一年四季都有不少游客，不过这几年因为家庭旅馆越来越多，有的家庭旅馆常常没人去住。可是陈先生的家庭旅馆差不多每天都没有空房间。为什么呢？

    原来陈先生家的房间虽然不大，可是特别干净，而且游客还可以上网。给游客做的早饭味道也很好，很有大理的特色。游客吃完早饭，陈先生就开车送他们去附近的景点。另外，游客离开的时候，陈先生还送给每人一件纪念品。这样陈先生陈太太和不少游客成了朋友，这些游客很高兴也很愿意把他们的家庭旅馆介绍给别人，所以来住的游客就越来越多了。下个月你去大理玩儿，去那儿住两天，就会看到他们和别的家庭旅馆不一样的地方了。

我認識大理的一位陳先生，他和太太開家庭旅館。大理附近的旅遊景點很多，一年四季都有不少遊客，不過這幾年因為家庭旅館越來越多，有的家庭旅館常常沒人去住。可是陳先生的家庭旅館差不多每天都沒有空房間。為什麼呢？

　　原來陳先生家的房間雖然不大，可是特別乾淨，而且遊客還可以上網。給遊客做的早飯味道也很好，很有大理的特色。遊客吃完早飯，陳先生就開車送他們去附近的景點。另外，遊客離開的時候，陳先生還送給每人一件紀念品。這樣陳先生陳太太和不少遊客成了朋友，這些遊客很高興也很願意把他們的家庭旅館介紹給別人，所以來住的遊客就越來越多了。下個月你去大理玩兒，去那兒住兩天，就會看到他們和別的家庭旅館不一樣的地方了。

1 ____ Mr. and Mrs. Chen own a bed-and-breakfast in Dali.

2 ____ Dali is a famous tourist destination, and business has been booming for all the bed-and-breakfasts there in recent years.

3 ____ The included breakfast features all the usual international choices.

4 ____ After breakfast, guests don't have to worry about transportation to the nearby scenic spots.

D Based on the passage in (C), circle the most appropriate choice. INTERPRETIVE

1 The Chens' bed-and-breakfast has an excellent reputation because it offers

　a　good prices, Internet access, free souvenirs, and transportation to nearby tourist spots.

　b　Internet access, transportation to nearby tourist spots, a good breakfast, and large rooms.

　c　clean rooms, a good breakfast, transportation to nearby tourist spots, and free souvenirs.

2 What can be said of the intended readers of this passage?

　a　They are curious about bed-and-breakfasts in Dali, but don't intend to visit.

　b　They are planning to travel to Dali and need a place to stay.

　c　They are interested in getting to know the reasons for the Chens' success.

E Read this passage, then mark the statements true or false. INTERPRETIVE

　　朋友，您生活在热闹的大城市上海，每天看到的都是高楼汽车，会不会担心有中国传统特色的东西越来越少了呢？想不想去看一个保留了很多传统建筑的古城？离上海不远的地方就有这样一个小小的古城，叫周庄 (Zhōuzhuāng)。周庄有九百多年的历史，很多房子都是一两百年前盖的，保留得很好。朋友，从上海来游览周庄吧！坐在周庄安静的茶馆里，一边喝茶，一边看外边的小河和门旁的红灯笼，您会觉得这是一次最好的旅游。如果您想报名参加我们的旅游团，请打8294-5832。团费150元，包括交通，午餐和景点门票。

朋友，您生活在熱鬧的大城市上海，每天看到的都是高樓汽車，會不會擔心有中國傳統特色的東西越來越少了呢？想不想去看一個保留了很多傳統建築的古城？離上海不遠的地方就有這樣一個小小的古城，叫周莊 (Zhōuzhuāng)。周莊有九百多年的歷史，很多房子都是一兩百年前蓋的，保留得很好。朋友，從上海來遊覽周莊吧！坐在周莊安靜的茶館裡，一邊喝茶，一邊看外邊的小河和門旁的紅燈籠，您會覺得這是一次最好的旅遊。如果您想報名參加我們的旅遊團，請打8294-5832。團費150元，包括交通，午餐和景點門票。

1 ____ This is an advertisement that would most likely be found in Zhouzhuang.

2 ____ People from Shanghai started visiting Zhouzhuang over nine hundred years ago.

3 ____ Many houses in Zhouzhuang are one or two hundred years old but are still in good shape.

4 ____ The writer implies that Shanghai is in danger of losing its Chinese character.

5 ____ According to the advertisement, the ambience of Zhouzhuang's teahouses will make you feel that it's the best trip you've ever taken.

F | Based on the passage in (E), circle the most appropriate choice.

1 In the advertisement, what is presented as Zhouzhuang's primary selling point?

   a its proximity to Shanghai

   b its difference from Shanghai

   c its hospitality to tourists from Shanghai

2 What expenses are covered by the one hundred and fifty yuan paid for the group tour?

   a roundtrip transportation, one meal, and admission tickets

   b a bus ride to Zhouzhuang, lunch and tea, and admission tickets

   c a roundtrip bus ride, admission tickets, souvenirs, and lunch

Look at this advertisement and answer the questions in English. INTERPRETIVE

云南 双飞五日
（丽江、大理、昆明）
2610 元

雲南 雙飛五日
（麗江、大理、昆明）
2610 元

1 这个广告是什么样的公司贴的？

這個廣告是什麼樣的公司貼的？

_____

2 广告说什么，请你翻译成英文。

廣告說什麼，請你翻譯成英文。

_____

H Look at this sign and answer the question in English. INTERPRETIVE

报名准备室

報名準備室

学生考试以前来这个办公室做什么？

學生考試以前來這個辦公室做什麼？

_____

I Look at this travel agency advertisement. List at least three things in English that would attract you to sign up for a tour with the agency. INTERPRETIVE

* 丰富三至五星酒店随心选择
* 出发日期、停留天数自由决定
* 全国二十余个出发城市
* 自由行、半自助游、团队游
  不同度假方式
* 接送机、观光游、景点门票等
  可提前预订
* 独家推出香港自由行 PASS

* 豐富三至五星酒店隨心選擇
* 出發日期、停留天數自由決定
* 全國二十餘個出發城市
* 自由行、半自助遊、團隊遊
  不同渡假方式
* 接送機、觀光遊、景點門票等
  可提前預訂
* 獨家推出香港自由行 PASS

A Form a character by combining the given components as indicated. Then use that character to write a word, phrase, or short sentence.

1 左边一个"力气"的"力"，右边一个"口"，
左邊一個"力氣"的"力"，右邊一個"口"，
是 _____ 的 ____ 。

2 左边一个"石头"的"石"，右边一个"更"，
左邊一個"石頭"的"石"，右邊一個"更"，
是 _____ 的 ____ 。

3 左边一个"开车"的"车"，右边一个"欠钱"的"欠"，
左邊一個"開車"的"車"，右邊一個"欠錢"的"欠"，
是 _____ 的 ____ 。

4 左边一个"纟"，右边一个"自己"的"己"，
左邊一個"糸"，右邊一個"自己"的"己"，
是 _____ 的 ____ 。

5 上边一个竹字头，下边一个"望子成龙"的"龙"，
上邊一個竹字頭，下邊一個"望子成龍"的"龍"，
是 _____ 的 ____ 。

B Rewrite these sentences, following the example below. PRESENTATIONAL

丽莎对南京夫子庙的印象很深。→ 南京夫子庙给丽莎留下了很深的印象。

麗莎對南京夫子廟的印象很深。→ 南京夫子廟給麗莎留下了很深的印象。

1 雪梅的舅舅对柯林的印象很好。
   雪梅的舅舅對柯林的印象很好。

   _____

2 天明和丽莎对云南的印象很好。
   天明和麗莎對雲南的印象很好。

   _____

3 天明对南京城市的变化印象很深。
   天明對南京城市的變化印象很深。

   _____

4 雪梅对舅舅住的小区印象很不错。
   雪梅對舅舅住的小區印象很不錯。

   _____

C Based on the Lesson Texts and the prompts, indicate what the IC characters prefer. State each character's preference twice, following the example below. PRESENTATIONAL

   joining a tour   VS.   traveling on his own

张天明觉得参加旅行团没有自助游自由。
張天明覺得參加旅行團沒有自助遊自由。

张天明觉得自助游比参加旅行团自由。
張天明覺得自助遊比參加旅行團自由。

1

chatting online　　　　VS.　　　　chatting on the phone

_____

_____

2

having a happy childhood　　VS.　　being successful as an adult

_____

_____

3

spending the New Year
in the U.S.　　　VS.　　spending the Chinese
New Year in China

_____

_____

D Based on the Lesson Texts and the given information below, complete the statements by using
只好. PRESENTATIONAL

1　雪梅在北京找工作。快过年了，不能回家给爸妈拜年，
　　_____。

　　雪梅在北京找工作。快過年了，不能回家給爸媽拜年，
　　_____。

2　柯林、天明觉得旅游时买纪念品很浪费时间，可是他们
　　参加的是有购物的团，所以_____。

　　柯林、天明覺得旅遊時買紀念品很浪費時間，可是他們
　　參加的是有購物的團，所以_____。

3 天明、丽莎还想在南京街上边走边拍照，但表哥肚子饿
了，_____。

天明、麗莎還想在南京街上邊走邊拍照，但表哥肚子餓
了，_____。

E Based on the visual clues, give advice or issue a warning by using 千万/千萬, following the example below. **PRESENTATIONAL**

生病

生病的时候，千万别乱吃药。
生病的時候，千萬別亂吃藥。

1 找旅行团/找旅行團

_____

2 下出租车/下出租車

_____

3 过春节/過春節

_____

F Complete the sentences with 不过/不過 (no more than). PRESENTATIONAL

1

这家商店的衣服很便宜，一条牛仔裤＿＿＿＿＿＿＿＿＿。

這家商店的衣服很便宜，一條牛仔褲＿＿＿＿＿＿＿＿＿。

2

还早，你再坐一会儿吧。现在＿＿＿＿＿＿＿＿＿＿＿＿。

還早，你再坐一會兒吧。現在＿＿＿＿＿＿＿＿＿＿＿＿。

3

这栋楼不高，＿＿＿＿＿＿＿＿＿＿＿＿＿＿＿＿＿＿。

這棟樓不高，＿＿＿＿＿＿＿＿＿＿＿＿＿＿＿＿＿＿。

4

HARRISVILLE
Population: 1000

他的家乡不大，人口＿＿＿＿＿＿＿＿＿＿＿＿＿＿。

他的家鄉不大，人口＿＿＿＿＿＿＿＿＿＿＿＿＿＿。

G Translate these dialogues into Chinese. PRESENTATIONAL

1 **Person A:** Do you need a box lunch?

＿＿＿＿＿＿＿＿＿＿＿＿＿＿＿＿＿＿＿＿＿＿＿＿

Person B: Do you have vegetarian box lunches?

＿＿＿＿＿＿＿＿＿＿＿＿＿＿＿＿＿＿＿＿＿＿＿＿

Person A: Sorry, the vegetarian box lunches are sold out.

_____

Person B: What else do you have?

_____

Person A: We also have instant noodles.

_____

Person B: Then I'll buy instant noodles.

_____

2 **Person A:** Dad, would you like to sleep in the upper bunk or lower bunk? The upper bunk is quieter; you can have a good night's sleep. The lower bunk is more convenient.

_____

_____

Person B: Then I'll take the lower bunk. I brought an extra blanket. Do you need it?

_____

Person A: One blanket is enough for me.

_____

3 **Person A:** Hi, Mom. We've returned to Beijing from Yunnan.

_____

Person B: Is that so? How did you get to Yunnan?

_____

Person A: We signed up online and joined a tour group. Then we took a train to Kunming and waited for Xuemei and Ke Lin.

_____

_____

Person B: Did you buy "soft" sleeper tickets or "hard" sleeper tickets?

_____

Person A: We wanted to practice speaking Chinese with the other passengers, so Lisha and I bought two tickets for a hard sleeper.

_____

Person B: Which places did you go to?

_____

Person A: We went to the Stone Forest, Dali, and Lijiang. We also went to see the Great Snow Mountain.

_____

Person B: What was your impression of Yunnan?

_____

Person A: Yunnan was really interesting! The landscape of each place was different. There were many fun places we didn't have time to go to.

_____

_____

Person A: Next time, then.

_____

H Translate these email messages into Chinese. PRESENTATIONAL

1   Lisha:

I checked online. There are many places in Yunnan with beautiful scenery. We can do a self-guided tour:

The first day—the Stone Forest, staying at a three-star (三星级/三星級) hotel

The second day—Dali, visiting the Three Pagodas of Dali, staying at a four-star (四星级/四星級) hotel

The third day—Lijiang's Old City, staying at a family-run hotel

How do you feel about this? We'll take a train to Kunming first. Ke Lin and Xuemei would also like to go to Yunnan. We can meet up in Kunming.

Tianming

_____

_____

_____

2 Tianming:

I'd like to travel on our own, because we'd have more freedom. However, we just got to China—I think it'd be more convenient for us to join a tour group. This way we wouldn't have to book hotels, or buy admission tickets. If we went to a different place every day to travel on our own, it'd be very exhausting [we'd be very tired]. A tour group would have a tour guide to introduce us to Yunnan's architecture, clothes, and foods and help us learn about each ethnic group's customs. What do you say?

Lisha

I | Translate this passage into Chinese. PRESENTATIONAL

Last year we went to England and stayed at a family hotel. Behind the hotel, there was a stream. The hotel wasn't very big, but it was very quiet and very clean, too. The owner cooked home-style dishes for us. They tasted very nice. The owner said that the fish he made for us came from the stream behind the hotel, so it was very fresh.

J | Propose a three-, five-, or seven-day itinerary in Chinese for tourists visiting your hometown or your favorite place to visit. Make sure to include means of transportation, places to stay, scenic spots to visit, tour guide's area of expertise, fees that will be charged, etc. Title your itinerary 《[地方的名字]三（五、七）日游 / 三（五、七）日遊》. PRESENTATIONAL

K Write a story in Chinese based on the four images below. Make sure that your story has a beginning, middle, and end, and that the transition from one picture to the next is smooth and logical. PRESENTATIONAL

_____

_____

_____

_____

_____

_____

_____

_____

生活与健康
生活與健康
Lifestyle and Health

✓ Check off the following language functions as you learn how to:

[ ] Talk about various types of exercises

[ ] Outline some healthy eating habits

[ ] Compare exercise habits in China and the U.S.

[ ] Point out the importance of a balanced diet

[ ] Describe habits that could age people prematurely or harm their health

As you progress through the lesson, note other language functions you would like to learn.

_____

_____

_____

I. Listening Comprehension

Audio

A Listen to the Lesson Text audio, then mark these statements true or false. INTERPRETIVE

1 ____ Lisha tutors Li Wen in English in exchange for free rent.

2 ____ Lisha sees people exercising in the neighborhood every morning.

3 ____ Lisha got up very early this morning to take a walk.

4 ____ Lisha thinks weight is a very important indicator of one's health.

5 ____ Lisha and Li Wen have differing opinions on how much one should eat at each meal in order to stay healthy.

6 ____ Li Wen has not gotten enough sleep recently.

B Listen to the Workbook Dialogue audio, then mark these statements true or false. INTERPRETIVE

1 ____ The daughter has been having small dinners for a long time.

2 ____ The father categorically disagrees with the notion that people should eat small dinners.

3 ____ The daughter is scheduled to go to work at seven o'clock tonight.

4 ____ The father has never worked a night shift before.

5 ____ Despite her father's advice, the daughter decides not to eat more for dinner.

6 ____ According to the daughter, eating a lot of food is not equivalent to being truly nourished.

C Listen to the Workbook Narrative 1 audio, then mark these statements true or false. INTERPRETIVE

1 ____ Li Wen's parents usually do tai chi in the park, but haven't done it for a few days.

2 ____ Li Wen's parents usually skip tai chi when it rains.

3 ____ Li Wen woke up early this morning to study.

4 ____ Li Wen's parents skipped their tai chi session this morning.

D Listen to the Workbook Narrative 2 audio, then mark these statements true or false. INTERPRETIVE

1 ____ Not many young Chinese people practice tai chi.

2 ____ Most young people in China prefer to exercise at a faster pace.

3 ____ Going to the gym has become popular in China in recent years.

E ____ Listen to the Workbook Listening Rejoinder audio. After hearing the first speaker, select the best response from the four choices given by the second speaker. Indicate the letter of your choice. INTERPRETIVE

A Compare the pronunciations of the underlined characters in the two words or phrases given. Provide their initials in *pinyin*.

出门/出門 _____　　　　　　必须/必須 _____

B Compare the tones of the underlined characters in the two words or phrases given. Indicate the tones with 1 (first tone), 2 (second tone), 3 (third tone), 4 (fourth tone), or 0 (neutral tone).

注意 _____　　　　　　　　主意 _____

III. Speaking

A Practice asking and answering these questions. INTERPERSONAL

1 你做过瑜伽，打过太极拳吗？

　你做過瑜伽，打過太極拳嗎？

2 你觉得瑜伽与太极拳，哪一个的动作更美？

　你覺得瑜伽與太極拳，哪一個的動作更美？

3 你平常怎么注意身体健康？

　你平常怎麼注意身體健康？

4 你有什么不好的饮食或生活习惯？

　你有什麼不好的飲食或生活習慣？

B Practice speaking with these prompts. PRESENTATIONAL

1 请谈谈你平常怎么锻炼身体，包括多久锻炼一次，每次锻炼多长时间。

　請談談你平常怎麼鍛煉身體，包括多久鍛煉一次，每次鍛煉多長時間。

2 请谈谈你平常做得到做不到"早餐要吃好，午餐要吃饱，晚餐要吃少"。为什么？

请談談你平常做得到做不到"早餐要吃好，午餐要吃飽，晚餐要吃少"。為什麼？

3 Describe a lifestyle that you think would be ideal from the perspective of health and well-being.

A Write the characters, *pinyin*, and English equivalent of each new word formed. Guess the meaning, then use a dictionary to confirm.

1 "散步"的"散" + "心事"的"心"

→ 散 + 心 → _____ _____ _____

2 "退休"的"退" + "进步"的"步"
"退休"的"退" + "進步"的"步"

→ 退 + 步 → _____ _____ _____

3 "动作"的"作" + "文章"的"文"
"動作"的"作" + "文章"的"文"

→ 作 + 文 → _____ _____ _____

4 "可能"的"能" + "力气"的"力"
"可能"的"能" + "力氣"的"力"

→ 能 + 力 → _____ _____ _____

5 "补充"的"补" + "学习"的"习"
"補充"的"補" + "學習"的"習"

→ 补/補 + 习/習 → _____ _____ _____

老张，好久没收到你的电子邮件了，最近好吗？听说你正在计划开餐馆，一定很忙。

很多人以为开餐馆很容易。我觉得这就要看餐馆开在哪儿了。你的餐馆开在什么地方最好呢？我说说我的看法，给你一点儿建议。

如果你们那儿有一家受欢迎的健身房，你就把餐馆开在健身房旁边吧。这是我的经验，也是有道理的。为什么很多人不常去餐馆吃饭？不是因为他们没钱，而是因为他们怕吃多了会越来越胖，对身体没有好处。可是如果你的餐馆旁边就是健身房，他们吃完饭就去锻炼，或者锻炼以后来吃饭，就不会那么担心了。怎么样？我说的有道理吧？

老張，好久沒收到你的電子郵件了，最近好嗎？聽說你正在計劃開餐館，一定很忙。

很多人以為開餐館很容易。我覺得這就要看餐館開在哪兒了。你的餐館開在什麼地方最好呢？我說說我的看法，給你一點兒建議。

如果你們那兒有一家受歡迎的健身房，你就把餐館開在健身房旁邊吧。這是我的經驗，也是有道理的。為什麼很多人不常去餐館吃飯？不是因為他們沒錢，而是因為他們怕吃多了會越來越胖，對身體沒有好處。可是如果你的餐館旁邊就是健身房，他們吃完飯就去鍛煉，或者鍛煉以後來吃飯，就不會那麼擔心了。怎麼樣？我說的有道理吧？

1 ____ The writer and Old Zhang have exchanged emails frequently.

2 ____ Old Zhang has owned a restaurant for many years.

3 ____ According to the writer, running a restaurant is not necessarily easy.

4 ____ The writer is looking for a good gym to join.

Based on the passage in (B), circle the most appropriate choice. INTERPRETIVE

1 According to the writer, what is key to the success of a restaurant?

   a good location

   b good food

   c good service

2 The writer believes that customers will not worry too much about the health effects of restaurant food if

   a they don't eat too much every time they visit a restaurant.

   b they don't eat at restaurants too frequently.

   c they can exercise at a gym right before or after eating at a restaurant.

D Read this passage, then mark the statements true or false. INTERPRETIVE

　　毛明今年春天高中毕业，秋天就要上大学了。他学习很好，可是不喜欢运动，所以爸爸妈妈有点儿担心他的身体健康。毛明七月过生日那天，爸爸给他的礼物是一套运动服，妈妈送给他一个游戏软件，上面有"姚明 (Yáo Míng) 打篮球"几个字。姚明是一位很有名的篮球运动员。毛明玩了那个游戏以后，开始对篮球有点儿兴趣了。九月初，毛明去上大学了。十月三十号是爸爸妈妈结婚二十年的纪念日。那天，他们收到了毛明给他们的礼物。他们打开一看，原来是一张照片，后面有"毛明打篮球"几个字。爸爸妈妈高兴极了。他们看了那张照片以后，再也不为儿子的健康担心了。

　　毛明今年春天高中畢業，秋天就要上大學了。他學習很好，可是不喜歡運動，所以爸爸媽媽有點兒擔心他的身體健康。毛明七月過生日那天，爸爸給他的禮物是一套運動服，媽媽送給他一個遊戲軟件，上面有"姚明 (Yáo Míng) 打籃球"幾個字。姚明是一位很有名的籃球運動員。毛明玩了那個遊戲以後，開始對籃球有點兒興趣了。九月初，毛明去上大學了。十月三十號是爸爸媽媽結婚二十年的紀念日。那天，他們收到了毛明給他們的禮物。他們打開一看，原來是一張照片，後面有"毛明打籃球"幾個字。爸爸媽媽高興極了。他們看了那張照片以後，再也不為兒子的健康擔心了。

1 ___ Mao Ming's parents were concerned that Mao Ming wouldn't get into a good university.

2 ___ On Mao Ming's eighteenth birthday, his parents had birthday gifts delivered to him at school.

3 ___ Mao Ming's parents have become more confident about their son's health.

E Based on the passage in (D), circle the most appropriate choice. INTERPRETIVE

1 Mao Ming's parents chose the birthday presents

    a based on Mao Ming's interests.

    b to get Mao Ming interested in sports.

    c based on their own love of sports.

2 What did Mao Ming give his parents as a gift?

    a an autographed picture of Yao Ming

    b a framed picture of Mao Ming's graduation ceremony

    c a picture of Mao Ming playing basketball

F Look at this sign and answer the questions. INTERPERSONAL

1 这个早餐店的名字是什么？

  這個早餐店的名字是什麼？

_____

2 请上网查查这个名字的英文是什么意思？

  請上網查查這個名字的英文是什麼意思？

_____

3 如果在这家店吃早饭，你会点什么？

  如果在這家店吃早飯，你會點什麼？

_____

暑期留学生武术课开课通知

一、 报名选课时间及地点： 6 月 25 日至 7 月 20 日
（中午 1：00~2：00 或下午 3：30~5：30）前到足球场小
房报名。报名电话：

二、上课内容、时间及地点：
 1、太极拳：
  早上 6：20—7：10 或 下午 4：00—4：50 每周一至周五上课。
  6 月 29 日早上 6：20 在足球场上课。
 2、长拳、剑术：
  下午 1：30—2：20 或 下午 4：00—4：50 每周一至周五。
  6 月 29 日下午 1：30 在足球场上课。
 注：6 月 29 日以后来的外国同学可插班上课，随堂报名。

体育教学部
2009-6-25

暑期留學生武術課開課通知

一、 報名選課時間及地點： 6 月 25 日至 7 月 20 日
（中午 1：00~2：00 或下午 3：30~5：30）前到足球場小
房報名。報名電話：

二、上課內容、時間及地點：
 1、太極拳：
  早上 6：20—7：10 或 下午 4：00—4：50 每週一至週五上課。
  6 月 29 日早上 6：20 在足球場上課。
 2、長拳、劍術：
  下午 1：30—2：20 或 下午 4：00—4：50 每週一至週五。
  6 月 29 日下午 1：30 在足球場上課。
 注：6 月 29 日以後來的外國同學可插班上課，隨堂報名。

體育教學部
2009-6-25

1 太极拳有几个班？每次上课上多长时间？

 太極拳有幾個班？每次上課上多長時間？

_____

2 哪一天开始上课？在什么地方上课？

 哪一天開始上課？在什麼地方上課？

_____

3 谁可以报名参加这个太极拳班？

誰可以報名參加這個太極拳班？

_____

4 报名时间是从什么时候到什么时候？

報名時間是從什麼時候到什麼時候？

_____

V. Writing and Grammar

A Form a character by combining the given components as indicated. Then use that character to write a word, phrase, or short sentence.

1 左边一个三点水，右边一个"主要"的"主"，

左邊一個三點水，右邊一個"主要"的"主"，

是 _____ 的 ____ 。

2 左边一个人字旁，右边一个"木"，

左邊一個人字旁，右邊一個"木"，

是 _____ 的 ____ 。

3 左边一个人字旁，右边一个"加州"的"加"，

左邊一個人字旁，右邊一個"加州"的"加"，

是 _____ 的 ____ 。

4 左边一个食字旁，右边一个"包"，

左邊一個食字旁，右邊一個"包"，

是 _____ 的 ____ 。

5 左边一个"口"，右边一个"来不及"的"及"，

左邊一個"口"，右邊一個"來不及"的"及"，

是 _____ 的 ____ 。

6 左边一个"目"，右边一个"民以食为天"的"民"，

左邊一個"目"，右邊一個"民以食為天"的"民"，

是 _____ 的 ____ 。

B Based on the prompts, give encouragement using 只要…就…, following the example below.
INTERPERSONAL

Person A: 我打太极拳动作不太美。
我打太極拳動作不太美。

Person B: 只要多打，动作就会好看。
只要多打，動作就會好看。

1 Person A: 我的身体不太好。
我的身體不太好。

Person B: _____。

2 Person A: 我做瑜伽的时候，动作常常会忘。
我做瑜伽的時候，動作常常會忘。

Person B: _____。

3 Person A: 我请了英文家教，可是英文还是进步不大。
我請了英文家教，可是英文還是進步不大。

Person B: _____。

C Little Ling is extremely easygoing. Friends do what they do, and it's all fine with him. Based on the images, pretend to be Little Ling and practice expressing how easygoing you are. Use 随便/隨便, following the example below. PRESENTATIONAL

别客气，冰箱里的水果你随便吃。
別客氣，冰箱裡的水果你隨便吃。

1

_____

_____

2

_____

_____

D | Little Ming, on the other hand, is not so easygoing. Based on the images, pretend to be Little Ming and practice expressing what isn't okay with you. Use 随便/隨便, following the example below.

PRESENTATIONAL

我的车请你别随便开。

我的車請你別隨便開。

1

_____

_____

2

_____

_____

E Based on the prompts, use 即使⋯也⋯ to express your determination to do something despite potential risks or disadvantages, following the example below. **INTERPERSONAL**

Person A: 你不要住校外，因为不太安全。
你不要住校外，因為不太安全。

Person B: 即使不太安全，我也要住校外。
即使不太安全，我也要住校外。

1 Person A: 冬天哈尔滨很冷，最好别去。
冬天哈爾濱很冷，最好別去。

Person B: _____。

2 Person A: 坐船游览长江，很花时间，还是算了吧。
坐船遊覽長江，很花時間，還是算了吧。

Person B: _____。

3 Person A: 春节夫子庙那儿人山人海，太挤了。我们在家玩游戏，怎么样？
春節夫子廟那兒人山人海，太擠了。我們在家玩遊戲，怎麼樣？

Person B: _____。

4 Person A: 这套运动服得花你一个月的工资，你非买不可吗？
這套運動服得花你一個月的工資，你非買不可嗎？

Person B: _____。

5   Person A: 听说这门金融课实在难学，我决定不选了，你
                还想选吗？

                聽說這門金融課實在難學，我決定不選了，你
                還想選嗎？

    Person B: _____。

F Based on the Lesson Texts and the prompts, imagine how the IC characters would give advice or issue a warning using 要不然, following the example below. PRESENTATIONAL

Tianming being late

丽莎告诉天明千万别迟到，要不然她会生气。
麗莎告訴天明千萬別遲到，要不然她會生氣。

1

Li Wen staying up late

_____

2

purchasing a soft-sleeper berth ticket

_____

3   joining a "shopping" tour

_____

G Translate these dialogues into Chinese. PRESENTATIONAL

1   **Person A:**   Old Li, you should pay more attention to your health and exercise.

_____

    Person B: Doctor, my house is too far away from the gym. Going to the gym is too inconvenient.

_____

    Person A: As long as you exercise, it doesn't matter where. You don't need to go to the gym. For example, you can do yoga at home.

_____

_____

    Person B: I'm an old man. It's a bit weird for me to do yoga.

_____

    Person A: Old Li, your thinking is problematic. OK, if you don't feel like doing yoga, you can go downstairs and practice tai chi.

_____

    Person B: Tai chi's movements are too slow. Besides, I won't be able to learn it.

_____

    Person A: Then how about jogging? You won't have to learn how to jog.

_____

    Person B: On the streets, there are cars everywhere. It's unsafe. Our residential development is too small. There's no place to jog.

_____

_____

Person A: Taking a walk is also a great exercise.

_____

Person B: I'll consider walking.

_____

2 Person A: Old Li, I see that you're much healthier.

_____

Person B: Doctor, I listened to your advice. Every morning I take a walk.

_____

Person A: I see that you're not as overweight as before.

_____

Person B: I used to eat a lot of meat and would seldom eat green leafy vegetables and fruit. I never had breakfast, ate anything I could find for lunch, and had a very big dinner. Now, besides taking a walk every day, I've also begun to pay attention to my diet.

_____

_____

_____

Person A: That's great. Now you have an excellent lifestyle. That's good for your health.

_____

3 Person A: Have you seen many older Chinese people exercising in the morning in public squares and parks?

_____

Person B: No. Since I came to China, I've been staying up late. Look at my panda eyes.

_____

Person A: I like to go to bed early and get up early. After breakfast, I go out and do tai chi.

_____

Person B: I should be like you and have a good lifestyle. I have seen older people dancing in public squares in the evening. It's really interesting.

_____

_____

Person A: You're right. In my country, generally speaking, everyone pays to go to a gym to exercise by themselves. It's both expensive and boring.

_____

_____

Person B: I agree. It's the same in my country. Older Chinese people exercising in public squares with friends—how great that is! It doesn't cost any money and you can meet old friends!

_____

_____

H Translate these passages into Chinese. PRESENTATIONAL

1   Lin Xuemei's uncle and aunt place a lot of importance on exercising. Ke Lin saw Lin Xuemei's uncle going to the small park in the residential development every morning to do tai chi and asked Uncle to teach him. Uncle told Ke Lin that he has been doing tai chi for ten years. Auntie, on the other hand, likes to do yoga in the evenings. Lin Xuemei did yoga together with Auntie. Ke Lin and Lin Xuemei both said that they had not only eaten well at Uncle's house, but they also learned to pay attention to their health.

_____

_____

_____

_____

_____

_____

_____

_____

2 Doctor, this is my dog Lele (乐乐/樂樂). You see, it's very fat. It eats a lot every day and doesn't like to drink water. Its eating habits are very bad, and it's lazy and doesn't like to exercise, so it has many health problems. My sister says this is because my lifestyle is not very good, either. She says I should exercise more and pay attention to my diet. She asks me to take Feifei jogging every day. Some people say that dogs resemble their owners (主人), but my sister says I have to pay attention; otherwise I'll resemble Feifei more and more.

_____

_____

_____

_____

_____

_____

_____

_____

I Compare your and Lisha's views on diet, lifestyle, and fitness. Comment on whether you would like to make any changes to improve your lifestyle, or whether you have any advice for Lisha.

PRESENTATIONAL

J Write a story in Chinese based on the four images below. Make sure that your story has a beginning, middle, and end, and that the transition from one picture to the next is smooth and logical. PRESENTATIONAL

1

2

3

4

_____

_____

_____

_____

_____

_____

_____

_____

_____

男女平等
Gender Equality

✓ Check off the following language functions as you learn how to:

[ ] Talk about equal treatment in relationships

[ ] Discuss gender equality in the workplace

[ ] Summarize the changes in Chinese women's social status since 1950

[ ] Describe how couples share household chores

As you progress through the lesson, note other language functions you would like to learn.

_____

_____

_____

I. Listening Comprehension

A Listen to the Lesson Text audio, then mark these statements true or false. INTERPRETIVE

1 ____ Women had a much lower status than men in traditional Chinese society, even though they were more or less equal to men in the family.

2 ____ There was significant improvement in women's social and familial status after 1950. More recently, however, there has been some regression.

3 ____ In modern China, men and women are more equal in the family than in the workplace.

4 ____ Xuemei's uncle and aunt split up the household chores.

5 ____ Xuemei's aunt is a fan of the Chinese men's soccer team.

6 ____ Xuemei's uncle is proud of the Chinese men's soccer team's victory over the world champion.

B Listen to the Workbook Dialogue audio, then mark these statements true or false. INTERPRETIVE

1 ____ The speakers have been living in the same neighborhood as Professor Qian and her husband since last year.

2 ____ The female speaker went to graduate school.

3 ____ The male speaker assumes that distinguished professors are usually over forty.

4 ____ Professor Qian does all kinds of household chores except dishwashing.

5 ____ The male speaker thinks both Professor Qian and her husband are happy in their marriage.

C Listen to the Workbook Narrative 1 audio, then mark these statements true or false. INTERPRETIVE

1 ____ The speaker doesn't like the men's soccer team.

2 ____ The woman will watch the soccer game on TV this evening.

3 ____ The speaker thinks that the members of the men's soccer team should return to college for further studies.

D Listen to the Workbook Narrative 2 audio, then circle the most appropriate choice. INTERPRETIVE

1 What is Li Xiaoyang's relationship with the speaker and the speaker's sister?

  a He is the speaker's friend and the speaker's sister's classmate.

  b He is the speaker's former classmate and the speaker's sister's fiancé.

  c He is the speaker's former classmate and the speaker's sister's friend.

2 What is the purpose of the speaker's message to his sister?

  a He wants her to reconsider her decision to marry.

  b He wants her to talk to her female classmates more.

  c He wants her to reevaluate her friendship with Li Xiaoyang.

3   What is the speaker's impression of Li Xiaoyang?

    a   Li Xiaoyang is sexist, and often argued with his female classmates in high school.

    b   Li Xiaoyang had many girlfriends in high school and is not to be trusted.

    c   In high school, Li Xiaoyang seemed arrogant and aloof because he seldom talked to girls.

4   How well does the speaker know Li Xiaoyang now?

    a   He knows him well because they see each other often.

    b   He doesn't know him well because they don't see each other often.

    c   He knows him well even though they don't see each other often.

E ____ Listen to the Workbook Listening Rejoinder audio. After hearing the first speaker, select the best response from the four choices given by the second speaker. Indicate the letter of your choice. INTERPRETIVE

II. Pinyin and Tone

A Compare the pronunciations of the underlined characters in the two words or phrases given. Provide their initials in *pinyin*.

输了/輸了 _____   需要 _____

B Compare the tones of the underlined characters in the two words or phrases given. Indicate the tones with 1 (first tone), 2 (second tone), 3 (third tone), 4 (fourth tone), or 0 (neutral tone).

情况/情況 _____   清淡 _____

III. Speaking

A Practice asking and answering these questions. INTERPERSONAL

1   你平常在家做什么家务?

    你平常在家做什麼家務?

2   在你们的国家，女性的家庭地位与社会地位跟男性一样吗?

    在你們的國家，女性的家庭地位與社會地位跟男性一樣嗎?

1 请谈谈对你来说什么样的夫妻是"模范夫妻"。

请談談對你來說什麼樣的夫妻是"模範夫妻"。

2 请谈谈在工作单位中有什么男女不平等的现象。

請談談在工作單位中有什麼男女不平等的現象。

3 Talk about what individuals and society can do about gender inequality.

IV. Reading Comprehension

A Write the characters, *pinyin*, and English equivalent of each new word formed. Guess the meaning, then use a dictionary to confirm.

1 "企业"的"企"＋"图书馆"的"图"

"企業"的"企"＋"圖書館"的"圖"

→ 企＋图/圖→ _____ _____ _____

2 "工厂"的"厂"＋"房子"的"房"

"工廠"的"廠"＋"房子"的"房"

→ 厂/廠＋房/房→ _____ _____ _____

3 "事情"的"事"＋"家务"的"务"

"事情"的"事"＋"家務"的"務"

→ 事＋务/務→ _____ _____ _____

4 "表现"的"表"＋"明白"的"明"

"表現"的"表"＋"明白"的"明"

→ 表＋明→ _____ _____ _____

5 "骄傲"的"傲"＋"快慢"的"慢"

"驕傲"的"傲"＋"快慢"的"慢"

→ 傲＋慢→ _____ _____ _____

B Draw a line connecting each noun or noun phrase on the left with an adjective on the right to form descriptions of the Chinese men's soccer team. **INTERPRETIVE**

1 社会地位/社會地位   a 骄傲/驕傲

2 家务事/家務事   b 糟糕

3 比赛成绩/比賽成績   c 高

4 态度/態度   d 多

C Read this passage, then mark the statements true or false. **INTERPRETIVE**

　　兰兰今年夏天大学毕业了。她有个哥哥，比她大两岁，高中毕业后没考上大学，就去开出租车了。兰兰的学习成绩比哥哥好，高中毕业后考进了一个名牌大学。她的父母薪水都不高，所以哥哥挣的钱差不多都给兰兰付学费了。好不容易等到兰兰大学毕业了，大家都以为她很快就会找到工作，没想到好几次面试后，都没拿到工作。虽然现在每个人都说男女应该平等，可是女大学毕业生找工作往往比男生难得多，因为不少单位担心女性结婚以后生孩子会影响工作。兰兰觉得很不公平。她想："要是女性都不结婚不生孩子，那将来社会上的工作谁来做啊？"

　　蘭蘭今年夏天大學畢業了。她有個哥哥，比她大兩歲，高中畢業後沒考上大學，就去開出租車了。蘭蘭的學習成績比哥哥好，高中畢業後考進了一個名牌大學。她的父母薪水都不高，所以哥哥掙的錢差不多都給蘭蘭付學費了。好不容易等到蘭蘭大學畢業了，大家都以為她很快就會找到工作，沒想到好幾次面試後，都沒拿到工作。雖然現在每個人都說男女應該平等，可是女大學畢業生找工作往往比男生難得多，因為不少單位擔心女性結婚以後生孩子會影響工作。蘭蘭覺得很不公平。她想："要是女性都不結婚不生孩子，那將來社會上的工作誰來做啊？"

1 ____ In high school, Lanlan was a better student than her brother.

2 ____ Lanlan went to university and her brother became a taxi driver.

3 ____ Lanlan's brother helped her pay for her tuition.

4 ____ Lanlan's family had expected that it would be difficult for Lanlan to find a job.

D Based on the passage in (C), circle the most appropriate choice. INTERPRETIVE

1 According to the passage, what is the primary reason that some employers are reluctant to hire female college graduates?

a They don't believe that female college graduates are as capable as their male counterparts.

b They are unwilling to offer the same salary to female and male college graduates.

c They are concerned that female employees' work will eventually be affected by their family responsibilities.

2 Which of the following statements is the most accurate?

a Lanlan has decided to not marry or have children.

b Lanlan wishes that she will have a son instead of a daughter in the future.

c Lanlan believes that women are unfairly punished for their social obligations.

E Read this passage, then mark each statement true or false. INTERPRETIVE

中国在历史上是个重男轻女的社会。虽然最近几十年，女性的家庭地位和社会地位都有了很大的提高，可是有些地方还有重男轻女的现象。比方说在农村，不少夫妻希望生男孩，不想要女孩，结果中国的男孩比女孩多了。这是一个很大的问题，中国政府要想出好办法才能解决。但是我觉得这可能也是一件好事儿。为什么呢？因为中国社会重男轻女的情况很快就要发生大变化了。你想，再过十几年到二十年，现在五、六岁的孩子要结婚的时候，很多男的都会担心找不到妻子。这样，谁还能重男轻女啊？

中國在歷史上是個重男輕女的社會。雖然最近幾十年，女性的家庭地位和社會地位都有了很大的提高，可是有些地方還有重男輕女的現象。比方說在農村，不少夫妻希望生男孩，不想要女孩，結果中國的男孩比女孩多了。這是一個很大的問題，中國政府要想出好辦法才能解決。但是我覺得這可能也是一件好事兒。為什麼呢？因為中國社會重男輕女的情況很快就要發生大變化了。你想，再過十幾年到二十年，現在五、六歲的孩子要結婚的時候，很多男的都會擔心找不到妻子。這樣，誰還能重男輕女啊？

1 ____ According to the writer, the problem of gender inequality is deeply rooted in Chinese history.

2 ____ According to the writer, improvements in women's status over the last few decades have been completely reversed in recent years.

3 ____ The writer assumes that the problem of gender imbalance in the population is largely confined to the upcoming generation.

4 ____ The writer believes that the status of Chinese women will improve significantly over the next two decades.

F Based on the passage in (E), circle the most appropriate choice. INTERPRETIVE

1 Which of the following is considered the primary reason for the imbalance between boys and girls?

a the preference for boys in many families

b the difficulty young men have in finding women to marry

c the side effect of government policy

2 Which statement best summarizes the passage's perspective?

a It is shocking that some people in contemporary China still consider men superior to women.

b It is mind-boggling that there are so many more boys than girls in contemporary China.

c It is ironic that the gender imbalance in China's population could present an opportunity for improving women's status.

G Look at this advertisement, then answer the questions in English. INTERPRETIVE

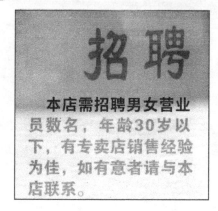 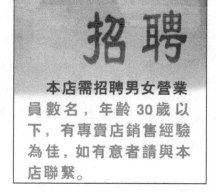

1 这份工作什么人可以申请?

這份工作什麼人可以申請?

_____

2 你对这份工作有兴趣吗? 为什么?

你對這份工作有興趣嗎? 為什麼?

_____

V. Writing and Grammar

A Form a character by combining the given components as indicated. Then use that character to write a word, phrase, or short sentence.

1 上边一个"田"，下边一个"力气"的"力"，
上邊一個"田"，下邊一個"力氣"的"力"，
是 ＿＿＿＿＿＿ 的 ＿＿＿ 。

2 左边一个"酉"，右边一个"加州"的"州"，
左邊一個"酉"，右邊一個"加州"的"州"，
是 ＿＿＿＿＿＿ 的 ＿＿＿ 。

3 左边一个"王"，右边一个"见"，
左邊一個"王"，右邊一個"見"，
是 ＿＿＿＿＿＿ 的 ＿＿＿ 。

4 上边一个"自己"的"自"，下边一个"心事"的"心"，
上邊一個"自己"的"自"，下邊一個"心事"的"心"，
是 ＿＿＿＿＿＿ 的 ＿＿＿ 。

5 左边一个人字旁，右边一个"言"，
左邊一個人字旁，右邊一個"言"，
是 ＿＿＿＿＿＿ 的 ＿＿＿ 。

Give reassuring answers by using the "是…的" construction, following the example below.

Q: 你说男女会平等吗?
你說男女會平等嗎?

A: 我相信有一天男女是会平等的。
我相信有一天男女是會平等的。

1 Q: 你认为工厂的问题能解决吗?
你認為工廠的問題能解決嗎?

A: _____。

2 Q: 你觉得他们夫妻二人的生活越来越好吗?
你覺得他們夫妻二人的生活越來越好嗎?

A: _____。

3 Q: 这种汤有营养吗?
這種湯有營養嗎?

A: _____。

4 Q: 世界各种比赛都很公平吗?
世界各種比賽都很公平嗎?

A: _____。

Based on the Lesson Texts, introduce an example by using 拿⋯来说/拿⋯來說, following the example below. PRESENTATIONAL

Some students who have scholarships also work part-time jobs.

很多有奖学金的学生也打工。拿丽莎来说吧，她就打工。
很多有獎學金的學生也打工。拿麗莎來說吧，她就打工。

1 Many first-year students live in the dorms.

_____

2 Some people think there is a lot of garbage online.

_____

3 Some people love buying souvenirs at tourist sights.

_____

4 Many couples share household chores.

_____

D Rewrite the following sentences using the "adjective + 得 + 不得了" structure, following the example below. **PRESENTATIONAL**

雪梅舅舅的英文非常非常棒。→ 雪梅舅舅的英文棒得不得了。

雪梅舅舅的英文非常非常棒。→ 雪梅舅舅的英文棒得不得了。

1 那家饭馆的菜很咸很咸。

那家飯館的菜很鹹很鹹。

_____

2 中国除夕夜非常非常热闹。

中國除夕夜非常非常熱鬧。

_____

3 这个古城保留的传统建筑非常非常多。

這個古城保留的傳統建築非常非常多。

_____

4 雪梅的舅舅对舅妈非常非常好。

雪梅的舅舅對舅媽非常非常好。

_____

5 放假的时候，中国各大旅游景点都非常非常挤。

放假的時候，中國各大旅遊景點都非常非常擠。

_____

E Convert these fractions into Chinese, following the example below. PRESENTATIONAL

1/10 　　　　十分之一

1 1/2 ＿＿＿＿＿＿＿＿＿＿＿＿＿＿

2 2/3 ＿＿＿＿＿＿＿＿＿＿＿＿＿＿

3 7/8 ＿＿＿＿＿＿＿＿＿＿＿＿＿＿

4 100/100 ＿＿＿＿＿＿＿＿＿＿＿＿＿＿

F You and the IC characters are going to travel together, so you divide up the tasks of preparing for the trip. First, draw a line connecting each person with a task, then declare who will be handling what by using 由, following the example below. INTERPRETIVE & PRESENTATIONAL

我　　　　　　　　计划旅游路线/計劃旅遊路線

→ 旅游路线由我计划。

→ 旅遊路線由我計劃。

1  　　a 买火车票/買火車票

2  　　b 订旅馆/訂旅館

3  　　c 安排活动/安排活動

4  　　d 拍照片

1 _____

2 _____

3 _____

4 _____

G Translate these dialogues into Chinese. PRESENTATIONAL

1 **Person A:** I heard some company bought a women's soccer team. It seems women's soccer is gradually gaining in popularity.

_____

_____

Person B: Right! There are more and more women playing and watching the sport.

_____

2 **Salesperson:** What would you like to buy?

_____

Li Zhe: Next month is my niece's birthday. I'd like to buy her a present.

_____

Salesperson: How old is she?

_____

Li Zhe: She'll be nine next month.

_____

Salesperson: How about this panda (stuffed animal)? It's forty-percent off.

_____

Li Zhe: Ever since she was in elementary school, my niece has loved playing soccer. Why don't I buy her a new soccer ball?

_____

_____

Salesperson:	But she's a girl.

_____

Li Zhe:	What you're saying is unfair. This is a gender-equal society.

_____

Salesperson:	Sir, I'm sorry. I didn't mean it that way. You can get a soccer ball on the second floor.

_____

_____

3 | Person A: | Who will win today's soccer game? The Spanish team or the French team? |
|---|---|

_____

Person B:	Both of those teams used to be world champions. I think the score will be zero to zero.

_____

Person A:	But recently the Spanish team hasn't been performing well. They've been losing all the time. I think the French team will probably win.

_____

_____

H Translate these passages into Chinese. PRESENTATIONAL

1 Historically, Chinese society favored men over women. Many parents wanted boys. Most girls didn't have the opportunity to be educated. Women's family and social status was also lower than men's. The situation changed greatly after 1949. Especially in the cities, many women began to work. Today, China has many female doctors and teachers. However, China still has (the phenomenon of) gender inequality. For example, in the countryside, girls have fewer opportunities than boys to be educated. Generally speaking, women's income is also lower than men's.

_____

_____

_____

_____

_____

_____

_____

_____

_____

2   Gao Ming's (高明) sister-in-law's name is Wang Wenying (王文英). She is an immigrant from Hong Kong. After marriage, she became Gao Wang Wenying. Gao Ming asked Xuemei if women in Mainland China (中国大陆/中國大陸) also adopt their husbands' family names after marriage. Xuemei said they didn't, and neither would she if she gets married. She would still be called Lin Xuemei. Gao Ming said women adopting their husband's last name is a social custom (社会习惯/社會習慣) in Hong Kong.

_____

_____

_____

_____

_____

_____

_____

I   Are men and women equal in your community? Explain your perspective, and include observations you have made in environments such as the home, school, workplace, and other social settings.

PRESENTATIONAL

J Write a story in Chinese based on the four images below. Make sure that your story has a
beginning, middle, and end, and that the transition from one picture to the next is smooth
and logical. PRESENTATIONAL

1

2

3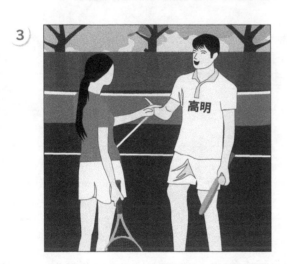

4

_____

_____

_____

_____

_____

_____

_____

_____

_____

Bringing It Together (Lessons 11–15)

I. Check Your Pronunciation

A Write down the correct pronunciation, including tones, of the following short sentences in *pinyin*. Use a computer or smartphone to record yourself speaking. If you've been asked to do so, send the recording to your teacher. Then translate each sentence into English. INTERPRETIVE

1 学期结束了，大家决定留在学校。

  學期結束了，大家決定留在學校。

  _____

  _____

2 吃年夜饭别忘了"年年有余"这句话。

  吃年夜飯別忘了"年年有餘"這句話。

  _____

  _____

3 中秋节是一家团圆的节日。

  中秋節是一家團圓的節日。

  _____

  _____

4 不是周末，没想到旅游景点挤满了车，挤满了游客。

  不是週末，沒想到旅遊景點擠滿了車，擠滿了遊客。

  _____

  _____

5 少数民族的建筑和服装都保留了很多传统特色。
  少數民族的建築和服裝都保留了很多傳統特色。

  _____

  _____

6 无论是硬卧还是软卧车厢，我都能睡得不错。
  無論是硬臥還是軟臥車廂，我都能睡得不錯。

  _____

  _____

7 我从来不喜欢自助游，都是参加旅行团。
  我從來不喜歡自助遊，都是參加旅行團。

  _____

  _____

8 高墙上挂着红灯笼，特别好看。
  高墙上掛著紅燈籠，特別好看。

  _____

  _____

9 买门票看熊猫的游客非常多。
  買門票看熊貓的遊客非常多。

  _____

  _____

10 那些退休夫妻早晨常在公园散步，有时候也打打太极拳。
那些退休夫妻早晨常在公園散步，有時候也打打太極拳。

_____

_____

11 熬夜的人必须补充睡眠，注意饮食，要不然容易生病。
熬夜的人必須補充睡眠，注意飲食，要不然容易生病。

_____

_____

12 大家都相信世界经济会逐渐变好。
大家都相信世界經濟會逐漸變好。

_____

_____

13 请注意发音：是"影响"，而不是"印象"。
請注意發音：是"影響"，而不是"印象"。

_____

_____

14 网上有消息说中国女足赢了世界冠军。
網上有消息說中國女足贏了世界冠軍。

_____

_____

II. Apply Your Chinese

A While studying abroad in China, you run into the following scenarios. PRESENTATIONAL

1 A Chinese family invites you to spend Chinese New Year with them. What would you say at New Year's Eve dinner?

_____

_____

_____

2 You are touring a Chinese city that has gone through a lot of transformations. What things would you say to express your astonishment about the contrast between the past and present?

_____

_____

_____

3 You want to tell your Chinese friends about your impression of a famous tourist destination you've just visited. What aspects would you touch upon?

_____

_____

_____

4 You are interested in people's dietary habits and workout routines. What would you say to your Chinese friends about the similarities and differences between what you see in China and what you see in your own country?

_____

_____

_____

5 You meet a group of young professionals who wish to learn about equal rights in the workplace in your country. What points would you bring up to explain the situation back home?

_____

_____

_____

A List a few things that Chinese people do to celebrate Chinese New Year. Rank these New Year's customs according to how much they appeal to you, with your favorite listed first. PRESENTATIONAL

1 _____

2 _____

3 _____

4 _____

5 _____

B List some interesting facts that you have learned about Nanjing. Rank them according to how much they impress you, with the most memorable listed first. PRESENTATIONAL

1 _____

2 _____

3 _____

4 _____

5 _____

C List the facts that you have learned about Yunnan. Rank them according to how interesting or useful they are to you, with the most noteworthy listed first. PRESENTATIONAL

1 _____

2 _____

3 _____

4 _____

5 _____

D List the forms of exercise that you would like to do in China. Rank them according to how eager you are to take part in them, with the one you want to do most listed first. PRESENTATIONAL

1 _____

2 _____

3 _____

4 _____

5 _____

E List the facts you have learned about gender roles in Chinese society. Rank them according to how interesting they are to you, with the most noteworthy listed first. PRESENTATIONAL

1 _____

2 _____

3 _____

4 _____

5 _____

IV. Summarize and Report

A Based on, but not limited to, the information you provided in (II) and (III), present an oral report or write a short essay in Chinese in response to each of the following questions. PRESENTATIONAL

1 Suppose you are going to host a Chinese New Year party. How would you prepare and decorate for the occasion? What would you say and offer to your guests?

2 Suppose you are going to make a documentary on the rise or decline of a town or city. What kinds of sights and sounds would reflect the changes? How would you dramatically present and narrate these changes?

3 Suppose you are organizing your own tour to Yunnan. What route would you choose, what places would you visit, and what do you need to know about those places?

4 Suppose you are a personal trainer. What would you say to encourage your clients to adopt healthier eating and exercise habits?

5 Suppose you are being interviewed by a Chinese graduate student in sociology about gender equality in your home country. What would you say about general attitudes toward gender relations in your country, and what examples would you give to support your arguments?

环境保护与节约能源
環境保護與節約能源

Environmental Protection and Energy Conservation

✓ Check off the following language functions as you learn how to:

[ ] Describe how to get close to and relax in nature

[ ] Talk about indicators of a clean environment

[ ] Discuss green and renewable energy

[ ] Explain what government can do to reduce pollution

[ ] Identify what individuals can do to protect the environment

As you progress through the lesson, note other language functions you would like to learn.

_____

_____

_____

A | Listen to the Lesson Text audio, then circle the most appropriate choice. INTERPRETIVE

1   How long had Zhang Tianming and his friends not seen each other?

   a   two or three months

   b   half a month

   c   a week

2   How do they get to the foot of the mountain?

   a   by bus

   b   by taxi

   c   by bicycle

3   Which temperature setting would violate the Chinese government's regulations on the use of heating and air-conditioning in public places?

   a   21 °C in winter

   b   26 °C in summer

   c   27 °C in summer

4   What change have some restaurants recently made regarding the use of chopsticks?

   a   They have started to use disposable chopsticks.

   b   They have stopped using disposable chopsticks.

   c   They now let the customers choose their chopsticks.

5   Why do people have to bring their own bags to the supermarket now?

   a   Shopping bags have become very expensive.

   b   Shopping bags are too small for their purchases.

   c   Shopping bags are a source of pollution.

6   According to Ke Lin, what should people start doing in their daily lives to protect the environment?

   a   drive less, walk more, and conserve more energy

   b   drive less, walk more, and stop buying bottled water

   c   drive less, walk more, and stop using air-conditioning

B | Listen to the Workbook Dialogue audio, then mark these statements true or false. INTERPRETIVE

1   ____   The woman is making a call from her car.

2   ____   When the woman went shopping, she hadn't yet heard about the supermarket's new policy.

3   ____   The man sounds supportive of the new policy.

4   ____   The woman asks the man to help carry the groceries because they are too heavy.

5   ____   The man decides not to drive because he doesn't think the woman really needs his help.

C Listen to the Workbook Narrative 1 audio, then circle the most appropriate choice. INTERPRETIVE

1 What is the speaker's current occupation?

   a   lumberjack

   b   student

   c   environmentalist

2 What dilemma does the speaker face?

   a   He can't decide whether to take a summer job or not.

   b   He can't decide whether to go back to school or not.

   c   He can't decide whether to speak to Little Lin or not.

3 The speaker needs Little Lin to tell him

   a   whether his summer job is environmentally friendly.

   b   how much next semester's tuition is.

   c   whether to take the summer job.

4 The speaker and Little Lin are probably

   a   husband and wife.

   b   friends.

   c   teacher and student.

D Listen to the Workbook Narrative 2 audio, then circle the most appropriate choice. INTERPRETIVE

1 What do you think is the relationship between the speaker and Xiaoming?

   a   father and son

   b   brother and sister

   c   professor and student

2 The speaker wants to make sure that

   a   Xiaoming won't forget to turn on the light in his room.

   b   Xiaoming won't forget to turn off the light in his room.

   c   he won't forget to turn off the light in Xiaoming's room

3 What is the speaker concerned about?

   a   high utility bills

   b   the frequency with which Xiaoming goes out

   c   environmental protection

E _____ Listen to the Workbook Listening Rejoinder audio. After hearing the first speaker, select the best response from the four choices given by the second speaker. Indicate the letter of your choice. INTERPRETIVE

A   Compare the pronunciations of the underlined characters in the two words or phrases given. Provide their initials in *pinyin*.

<u>塑</u>料袋 _____   树<u>下</u>边/樹<u>下</u>邊 _____

B   Compare the tones of the underlined characters in the two words or phrases given. Indicate the tones with 1 (first tone), 2 (second tone), 3 (third tone), 4 (fourth tone), or 0 (neutral tone).

砍<u>树</u>/砍<u>樹</u> _____   <u>看</u>书/<u>看</u>書 _____

III. Speaking

A   Practice asking and answering these questions. INTERPERSONAL

1   你住的地方空气污染严重吗？为什么？

     你住的地方空氣汙染嚴重嗎？為什麼？

2   你住的地方垃圾回收的工作顺利吗？为什么？

     你住的地方垃圾回收的工作順利嗎？為什麼？

3   除了爬山、骑自行车以外，你觉得还有什么样的活动有益于身体健康？

     除了爬山、騎自行車以外，你覺得還有什麼樣的活動有益於身體健康？

B   Practice speaking with these prompts. PRESENTATIONAL

1   请谈谈你怎么保护环境。

     請談談你怎麼保護環境。

2   请谈谈你怎么节约能源。

     請談談你怎麼節約能源。

3   The Chinese government has imposed regulations on the use of heating and air conditioning in public places. Do you think your government should come up with similar laws? Why or why not?

IV. Reading Comprehension

A Write the characters, *pinyin*, and English equivalent of each new word formed. Guess the meaning, then use a dictionary to confirm.

1   "资料"的"资" + "能源"的"源"

   "資料"的"資" + "能源"的"源"

   → 资/資 + 源 → _____ _____ _____

2   "有益"的"益" + "好处"的"处"

   "有益"的"益" + "好處"的"處"

   → 益 + 处/處 → _____ _____ _____

3   "一枝笔"的"笔" + "垃圾筒"的"筒"

   "一枝筆"的"筆" + "垃圾筒"的"筒"

   → 笔/筆 + 筒 → _____ _____ _____

4   "太阳"的"阳" + "农历"的"历"

   "太陽"的"陽" + "農曆"的"曆"

   → 阳/陽 + 历/曆 → _____ _____ _____

5   "身体"的"体" + "温度"的"温"

   "身體"的"體" + "溫度"的"溫"

   → 体/體 + 温/溫 → _____ _____ _____

B Draw a line connecting each verb on the left with its appropriate object on the right. Note that some of the verbs can be matched with more than one object. For this exercise, use the combinations that have been taught in the lessons so far. INTERPRETIVE

1	减轻/減輕	a	污染/汙染
2	保护/保護	b	能源
3	省	c	特色
4	减少/減少	d	环境/環境
5	保留	e	负担/負擔
6	节约/節約	f	钱/錢

C Read the passage, then mark the statements true or false. INTERPRETIVE

改革开放以来，中国经济发展得非常快，但是也造成了严重的环境污染。中国政府现在越来越重视环保问题了。一个办法是节约能源。政府已经规定，公共场所夏天空调的温度不能太低，冬天暖气的温度不能太高。另外一个办法是用太阳能和风能。很多中国家庭都用上了太阳能板，用太阳能发电，又省钱，又不污染环境。要是你坐火车去中国西部，可能会看到一个个风力发电机。中国已经成为用太阳能和风能最多的国家。

改革開放以來，中國經濟發展得非常快，但是也造成了嚴重的環境汙染。中國政府現在越來越重視環保問題了。一個辦法是節約能源。政府已經規定，公共場所夏天空調的溫度不能太低，冬天暖氣的溫度不能太高。另外一個辦法是用太陽能和風能。很多中國家庭都用上了太陽能板，用太陽能發電，又省錢，又不汙染環境。要是你坐火車去中國西部，可能會看到一個個風力發電機。中國已經成為用太陽能和風能最多的國家。

1 ____ The writer considers environmental damage in China to have resulted from rapid economic development.

2 ____ According to the writer, the Chinese government pays more attention to environmental protection now than it did before.

3 ____ Every household in China has to follow the government's rules regarding heating and air-conditioning.

4 ____ Renewable energy has become commonplace in China.

D Based on the passage in (C), circle the most appropriate choice. INTERPRETIVE

1 Which statement is most accurate?

    a China has more resources for solar and wind energy than any other country.

    b China is the world leader in solar and wind power generation.

    c Trains in China will soon be driven mostly by solar and wind energy.

E Read the passage, then mark the statements true or false. INTERPRETIVE

哥哥：

    我现在已经不在原来那家公司上班了。在那里，我的工作就是卖一次性筷子给日本、德国和美国等国家，卖得很好，公司很高兴，所以我的薪水也很不错。可是我每次拿薪水的时候，都要问自己：为了那些一次性筷子，我们砍了多少树啊？我的不少同学都在做环保工作，做有益于环境保护的事，可是我为了挣钱，老是做对环境没有好处的事。我这样一想，晚上就睡不好觉了，最后我决定不去那家公司上班了。你们不用为我担心，我会找到新的工作的。我现在找工作的标准是，不管薪水多少，一定是要有益于环保的。

妹妹

哥哥：

    我現在已經不在原來那家公司上班了。在那裡，我的工作就是賣一次性筷子給日本、德國和美國等國家，賣得很好，公司很高興，所以我的薪水也很不錯。可是我每次拿薪水的時候，都要問自己：為了那些一次性筷子，我們砍了多少樹啊？我的不少同學都在做環保工作，做有益於環境保護的事，可是我為了掙錢，老是做對環境沒有好處的事。我這樣一想，晚上就睡不好覺了，最後我決定不去那家公司上班了。你們不用為我擔心，我會找到新的工作的。我現在找工作的標準是，不管薪水多少，一定是要有益於環保的。

妹妹

1 ____ The writer is currently unemployed.

2 ____ The company that the writer worked for was engaged in a lucrative export business.

3 ____ The writer made a lot of money for the company but was not paid well.

4 ____ The writer had to work the night shift frequently and didn't get enough sleep.

F Based on the passage in (E), circle the most appropriate choice. INTERPRETIVE

1 Which of the statements is most accurate?

  a The writer is curious about how many trees are cut down to produce her former employer's products.

  b The writer feels guilty that so many trees are cut down to produce her former employer's products.

  c The writer marvels that so many trees are cut down to produce her former employer's products.

2 How does the writer feel when she thinks about what her former classmates are doing?

  a She is ashamed that she was doing the opposite of what they are doing.

  b She is glad that she was doing something similar to what they are doing.

  c She is indifferent to whether they are doing similar things or not.

3 For her next job, the writer will probably look for one that is

  a well paid and environmentally friendly

  b poorly paid but environmentally friendly

  c environmentally friendly, regardless of the pay

G Look at these signs, then answer the questions. INTERPRETIVE

1 请把这个商店的名字翻译成英文。

请把這個商店的名字翻譯成英文。

_____

2 请用英文写出它让你做什么。

请用英文寫出它讓你做什麼。

_____

> 请把食品 垃圾
> 扔在厨房垃圾筒!
> PLEASE PUT THE FOOD
> RUBISH IN THE KITCHEN!
> THANK YOU, 谢谢!

3 这句话应该怎样翻译才对?

這句話應該怎樣翻譯才對?

_____

> 保护水环境 人人 有 责

4 What's everyone's duty? Answer in English: _____

1 广告上说他们卖什么东西？请写出四种，并翻译成英文。
　广告上說他們賣什麼東西？請寫出四種，並翻譯成英文。

_____

2 他们还有什么服务让你觉得在那儿买东西很方便？请用
　英文写出来。
　他們還有什麼服務讓你覺得在那兒買東西很方便？請用
　英文寫出來。

_____

_____

V. Writing and Grammar

A Form a character by combining the given components as indicated. Then use that character to write a word, phrase, or short sentence.

1 左边一个三点水，右边一个"原来"的"原"，
　左邊一個三點水，右邊一個"原來"的"原"，
　是 _____ 的 _____ 。

2 左边一个提手旁，右边一个"隹"，
　左邊一個提手旁，右邊一個"隹"，
　是 _____ 的 _____ 。

3　上边一个竹字头，下边一个"快"，
　　上邊一個竹字頭，下邊一個"快"，
　　是 ＿＿＿＿＿＿ 的 ＿＿＿ 。

4　左边一个"夫子庙"的"夫"，右边一个"见面"的"见"，
　　左邊一個"夫子廟"的"夫"，右邊一個"見面"的"見"，
　　是 ＿＿＿＿＿＿ 的 ＿＿＿ 。

5　左边一个"石头"的"石"，右边一个"欠钱"的"欠"，
　　左邊一個"石頭"的"石"，右邊一個"欠錢"的"欠"，
　　是 ＿＿＿＿＿＿ 的 ＿＿＿ 。

B Based on the clues given, use the "Verb 1 的 verb 1, verb 2 的 verb 2" pattern to describe what the students, tourists, park visitors, and soccer fans are doing to contribute to the overall mood of each setting. Follow the example below. PRESENTATIONAL

library   quiet

图书馆里，学生看书的看书，睡觉的睡觉，很安静。
圖書館裡，學生看書的看書，睡覺的睡覺，很安靜。

1　Temple of Confucius　 　bustling

_____

2 park   fun

3 soccer field   joy

C Contemplate different alternatives using ⋯吧， ⋯吧, following the example below.
INTERPERSONAL

Q: 你打算怎么去听音乐会？
你打算怎麼去聽音樂會？

A: 坐出租车吧，太贵，走路吧，太远，我还是骑自行车去吧。
坐出租車吧，太貴，走路吧，太遠，我还是騎自行車去吧。

1

 $$$

Q: 你今天想买什么水果？
　　你今天想買什麼水果？

A: _____ 。

2

  $$$

Q: 你周末想做什么？
　　你週末想做什麼？

A: _____ 。

3

   $$$

Q: 小白明天过生日，你准备送什么礼物？
　　小白明天過生日，你準備送什麼禮物？

A: _____ 。

1 我们去年是什么时候去爬大雪山的？你 _____ 了吗？

  我們去年是什麼時候去爬大雪山的？你 _____ 了嗎？

2 大家还不知道怎么给爷爷过八十岁生日，希望能赶
  快 _____ 一个好主意。

  大家還不知道怎麼給爺爺過八十歲生日，希望能趕
  快 _____ 一個好主意。

3 她的手机号码你 _____ 以后，请告诉我。

  她的手機號碼你 _____ 以後，請告訴我。

4 柯林 _____ 一个去长城的好办法，又省钱又好玩儿。

  柯林 _____ 一個去長城的好辦法，又省錢又好玩兒。

5 叔叔在哪个企业单位工作我到现在还没 _____ 。

  叔叔在哪個企業單位工作我到現在還沒 _____ 。

E Draw a line connecting each activity on the left with its possible benefit on the right, then make a
statement based on each match using 有益于/有益於. INTERPRETIVE & PRESENTATIONAL

1 运动
  運動

a 环境保护
  環境保護

2 用太阳能或风能发电
  用太陽能或風能發電

b 减少白色污染
  減少白色汙染

3 不随便乱扔垃圾
  不隨便亂扔垃圾

c 身体健康
  身體健康

4 不用塑料袋

d 节约传统能源
  節約傳統能源

1 _____

2 _____

3 _____

4 _____

F Convert the following into Chinese using 于/於, following the example below. PRESENTATIONAL

3 > 2   三大于二/三大於二

1 8 < 9   _____

2 101 > 100   _____

3 2/3 > 1/2   _____

4 79 + 24 = 103 _____

5 1000 – 438 = 562 _____

G Write out the weather forecasts in Chinese, following the example below. PRESENTATIONAL

today   Beijing 15 °C   Nanjing 19 °C   北京今天的温度低于南京。
                                              北京今天的溫度低於南京。

1 tonight   Shenzhen 27 °C Tianjin 21 °C   _____

2 tomorrow   Shanghai 20 °C Hangzhou 22 °C   _____

3 yesterday   New York 70 °F Harbin 16 °C   _____

H Translate this dialogue into Chinese. PRESENTATIONAL

Person A: Your shirt looks really good. Where did you get it?

_____

Person B: It's an old shirt of my mom's. I got my furniture at a second-hand furniture store (旧家具店/舊傢俱店), too.

_____

_____

Person A: You are really thrifty.

_____

Person B: I'm still paying back my student loan. I don't have a lot of money. Besides, I feel that if old things are still usable, why buy new ones? Now I try my best to buy as few things as possible and waste as little as possible.

_____

_____

Person A: No wonder you are thrifty with paper, too.

_____

Person B: If we don't conserve and don't pay attention to recycling, the earth will have more and more trash.

_____

_____

Person A: I agree.

_____

I Translate these passages into Chinese. PRESENTATIONAL

1   "Protect the earth; protect our home." We will meet Thursday evening at 7:00 in Room 305 in Building No. 5 to discuss how environmental protection starts with small things and with each and every one of us. We welcome everybody to participate [in the meeting].

_____

_____

_____

_____

2   Let's protect the green earth and reduce white pollution together. Please conserve paper. Do not use disposable chopsticks. Do not drink bottled water. This weekend we will go to the outskirts of the city to plant trees (种树/種樹) and recycle plastic bags and plastic bottles. We welcome everybody to participate.

_____

_____

_____

_____

3   My cousin Tianliang (天亮) used to bike to work. Now he has started to drive. However, his girlfriend Xiaoqing (小青) feels that riding a bike can not only strengthen one's body but also save money. Furthermore, it is good for the environment. That's why she doesn't want to buy a car. She says that since he bought a car, Tianliang seldom exercises and has put on weight. Besides, there are so many cars on the streets. Driving is not as convenient as biking. Tianliang feels that what Xiaoqing says makes sense. He plans to sell his car, buy a bicycle, and bike to work with Xiaoqing.

_____

_____

_____

_____

_____

_____

_____

J   Translate this email from Tianming to his father. PRESENTATIONAL

Dad,

Yesterday my friends and I biked out of town to hike in the mountains. We saw many houses using solar energy to generate electricity. We thought it was really cool. After I got back to the dorm in the evening, I went online and did some research. It turns out that many places in China use solar and wind power to generate electricity. Currently, many countries in the world are having an energy crisis. Hopefully, solar and wind power will help the world solve the energy crisis.

Tianming

_____

_____

_____

_____

_____

K What lifestyle changes are people in your community making to protect the environment? Compile your observations as a report titled 《绿色生活/綠色生活》. PRESENTATIONAL

L Write a story in Chinese based on the four images below. Make sure that your story has a beginning, middle, and end, and that the transition from one picture to the next is smooth and logical. PRESENTATIONAL

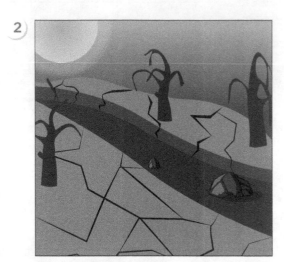

_____

_____

_____

_____

_____

第十七课

第十七課

理财与投资
理財與投資
Wealth Management and Investing

✓ Check off the following language functions as you learn how to:

[ ] Discuss whether you're a saver or a spender

[ ] Identify ways to invest money

[ ] List ways to purchase a big-ticket item

[ ] Describe your spending habits

[ ] Recount in basic terms the ups and downs of the stock market

As you progress through the lesson, note other language functions you would like to learn.

_____

_____

_____

A Listen to the Lesson Text audio, then circle the most appropriate choice. INTERPRETIVE

1 Many Chinese people have savings because

   a they are thrifty.

   b they flip stocks.

   c they speculate in real estate.

2 What did Zhang Tianming's aunt originally plan to do with her personal savings?

   a buy stocks

   b pay for her grandchildren's education

   c buy an apartment

3 Why don't Zhang Tianming's cousin and his fiancée let his mother buy a new car for them?

   a They already have a car.

   b Their workplaces are close to each other.

   c both of the above

4 Why did Zhang Tianming's aunt change her mind about buying a new apartment?

   a She heard she could make more money from stocks.

   b She heard real estate prices would go down.

   c She heard bank interest rates would go up.

5 What did Zhang Tianming's aunt ultimately decide to do with her money?

   a purchase an apartment

   b buy stocks

   c We do not know.

B Listen to the Workbook Dialogue audio, then mark these statements true or false. INTERPRETIVE

1 ____ The man made some money in the stock market in the past, but recently, he has lost money.

2 ____ The man is stressed because of the status of his investments.

3 ____ The man had wanted to invest in the stock market because he was very wealthy.

4 ____ The woman seems to know the stock market better than the man does.

5 ____ According to the woman, now is the best time to sell stocks.

6 ____ According to the woman, the stock market is not likely to stay the same for long.

C Listen to the Workbook Narrative 1 audio, then circle the most appropriate choice. INTERPRETIVE

1 The two speakers are most likely
  a wife and husband
  b mother and son
  c daughter and father

2 What is the female speaker's preferred way to manage wealth?
  a buying stocks
  b buying real estate
  c keeping money in a savings account

3 How did the male speaker decide to invest?
  a buy stocks
  b buy real estate
  c put the money into a savings account

4 Why is the female speaker worried?
  a The two speakers are retiring in three months but have lost a third of their money.
  b The two speakers are retiring in a few years but have lost a third of their money.
  c The two speakers have lost a third of their money over the past few years.

D Listen to the Workbook Narrative 2 audio, then mark these statements true or false. INTERPRETIVE

1 ____ The speaker leaves this voicemail for Daliang because Daliang's cell phone is off.

2 ____ The speaker and his wife plan to use their savings to apply for a mortgage loan.

3 ____ The speaker and his wife don't currently own any real estate.

4 ____ The speaker is certain that he and his wife will sign the contract next week.

E ____ Listen to the Workbook Listening Rejoinder audio. After hearing the first speaker, select the best response from the four choices given by the second speaker. Indicate the letter of your choice. INTERPRETIVE

II. Pinyin and Tone

A Compare the pronunciations of the underlined characters in the two words or phrases given. Provide their initials in *pinyin*.

存款 _____   纯棉／純棉 _____

B Compare the tones of the underlined characters in the two words or phrases given. Indicate the tones with 1 (first tone), 2 (second tone), 3 (third tone), 4 (fourth tone), or 0 (neutral tone).

房价<u>涨</u>/房價<u>漲</u> _____   一张<u>纸</u>/一張<u>紙</u> _____

III. Speaking

A Practice asking and answering these questions. INTERPERSONAL

1 你认为什么样的投资风险高？
   你認為什麼樣的投資風險高？

2 你认为怎样理财没有风险？为什么？
   你認為怎樣理財沒有風險？為什麼？

3 你认为父母需要为子女将来的教育费担心吗？为什么？
   你認為父母需要為子女將來的教育費擔心嗎？為什麼？

B Practice speaking with these prompts. PRESENTATIONAL

1 请谈谈如果你有一百万元，你会怎么投资。
   請談談如果你有一百萬元，你會怎麼投資。

2 你赞成省吃俭用地过日子，还是以"钱只有花了才是自己的"的态度过日子？为什么？
   你贊成省吃儉用地過日子，還是以"錢只有花了才是自己的"的態度過日子？為什麼？

3 Recap the story from the Lesson Text about the two elderly women, and explain the point of the story. Do you agree with the message? Why or why not?

A Write the characters, *pinyin*, and English equivalent of each new word formed. Guess the meaning, then use a dictionary to confirm.

1 "炒股"的"炒"+"方便面"的"面"

 "炒股"的"炒"+"方便麵"的"麵"

 → 炒 + 面/麵 → _____ _____ _____

2 "郁闷"的"闷"+"生气"的"气"

 "鬱悶"的"悶"+"生氣"的"氣"

 → 闷/悶 + 气/氣 → _____ _____ _____

3 "辛苦"的"苦"+"用功"的"功"

 "辛苦"的"苦"+"用功"的"功"

 → 苦/苦 + 功 → _____ _____ _____

4 "签合同"的"签"+"名字"的"字"

 "簽合同"的"簽"+"名字"的"字"

 → 签/簽 + 字 → _____ _____ _____

5 "突然"的"突"+"变化"的"变"

 "突然"的"突"+"變化"的"變"

 → 突 + 变/變 → _____ _____ _____

B Fill in the blanks with the words provided. INTERPRETIVE

讨论　　兴趣　　反对　　危机　　注意

1 旁边的几个朋友正在分享自己投资理财的经验，这引起小王的 _____。

2 导游的建议，有些人赞成，但也引起一些人的 _____。

3 在安静的病房里，突然有人的脚步声，引起了医生的
_____。

4 煤和石油越来越少，如果再不节能，恐怕会引起全世界
的能源_____。

5 张教授希望用报上的文章来引起大家对环保问题的
_____。

討論　　興趣　　反對　　危機　　注意

1 旁邊的幾個朋友正在分享自己投資理財的經驗，這引起
小王的_____。

2 導遊的建議，有些人贊成，但也引起一些人的
_____。

3 在安靜的病房裡，突然有人的腳步聲，引起了醫生的
_____。

4 煤和石油越來越少，如果再不節能，恐怕會引起全世界
的能源_____。

5 張教授希望用報上的文章來引起大家對環保問題的
_____。

C Read the passage, then mark the statements true or false. INTERPRETIVE

　　白先生和白太太夫妻倆收入很高。以前他們一直把钱存在银行里，安全是安全，可是利息太低，所以他们开始考虑用别的方式投资。白先生认为买房子好，可是白太太觉得炒股赚钱更快。他们谁也说服不了谁，只好用一半钱买了一套房子，把另一半钱放进股市里。从那以后，夫妻倆常吵架。房价涨的时候，白先生就说："要是我们不买股票，买两套房子，那多好啊。"股票涨的时候，白太太就说："要是我们不买房子，把钱都用来买股票，那多好

啊。"上个月，他们把房子和股票都卖了，把钱又存到银行里去了。现在，他们的钱涨得很慢，可是两个人不再吵架了。

白先生和白太太夫妻俩收入很高。以前他们一直把钱存在银行裡，安全是安全，可是利息太低，所以他们开始考虑用别的方式投资。白先生认为买房子好，可是白太太觉得炒股赚钱更快。他们谁也说服不了谁，只好用一半钱买了一套房子，把另一半钱放进股市裡。从那以后，夫妻俩常吵架。房价涨的时候，白先生就说："要是我们不买股票，买两套房子，那多好啊。"股票涨的时候，白太太就说："要是我们不买房子，把钱都用来买股票，那多好啊。"上个月，他们把房子和股票都卖了，把钱又存到银行裡去了。现在，他们的钱涨得很慢，可是两个人不再吵架了。

1 _____ In the past, Mr. and Mrs. Bai managed to build up their bank savings despite having little income.

2 _____ Mr. and Mrs. Bai agreed to withdraw their money from the bank, but couldn't agree on how to invest it.

3 _____ Tensions arose between Mr. and Mrs. Bai when their investments did not generate good returns.

4 _____ Now, Mr. and Mrs. Bai would probably say that putting their money in a savings account is good for maintaining marital harmony.

D Based on the passage in (C), circle the most appropriate choice. INTERPRETIVE

1 Which of the following best describes Mr. and Mrs. Bai's investments until last month?

a They invested half their money in real estate and the other half in stocks.

b Half of the time, they invested all their money in real estate; the other half of the time, they invested all their money in stocks.

c Half of their returns were from real estate and the other half were from stocks.

2 Which of the following statements is most accurate?

a Both the real estate market and the stock market were stagnant.

b Both real estate prices and stock prices were extremely volatile.

c The real estate market and the stock market both hit highs, but at different times.

3 Mr. and Mrs. Bai ultimately decided to go back to bank savings because

a the growth of their bank savings was slow but very steady.

b they couldn't agree on an investment strategy.

c neither of them was an aggressive investor.

表姐：

　　你告诉我你这几年挣了不少钱，我真的非常高兴。听舅舅舅妈说，你小时候他们收入不高，连给你买双新鞋的钱都没有。现在不一样了。你们有了大房子，也有了新车，还有了不少存款。我同意你说的，把钱存在银行里不是最好的投资理财方式。我知道舅舅舅妈一直想再买一套房子，等到房价涨的时候再卖出去。我也知道你自己觉得股票市场赚钱可能更容易。可是，除了房子和股市以外，就没有别的投资方式了吗？在你们家过春节的时候，我就注意到，你们那儿很多老年人早上在公园里打太极拳，可是二、三十岁的人没有很多锻炼身体的地方。所以我觉得，花钱开个健身房一定受欢迎，也一定会赚钱。我有个朋友在海南开健身房。要是你有兴趣，我可以让他跟你聊聊。

小静

表姐：

　　你告訴我你這幾年掙了不少錢，我真的非常高興。聽舅舅舅媽說，你小時候他們收入不高，連給你買雙新鞋的錢都沒有。現在不一樣了。你們有了大房子，也有了新車，還有了不少存款。我同意你說的，把錢存在銀行裡不是最好的投資理財方式。我知道舅舅舅媽一直想再買一套房子，等到房價漲的時候再賣出去。我也知道你自己覺得股票市場賺錢可能更容易。可是，除了房子和股市以外，就沒有別的投資方式了嗎？在你們家過春節的時候，我就注意到，你們那兒很多老年人早上在公園裡打太極拳，可是二、三十歲的人沒有很多鍛煉身體的地方。所以我覺得，花錢開個健身房一定受歡迎，也一定會賺錢。我有個朋友在海南開健身房。要是你有興趣，我可以讓他跟你聊聊。

小靜

1 ____ Xiaojing's cousin cannot afford to buy a pair of new shoes because all her money is in the bank.

2 ____ Xiaojing is happy to report that she has made a lot of money in recent years.

3 ____ Xiaojing and her cousin agree that putting money in the bank is not the best way to invest.

4 ____ Xiaojing's uncle and aunt hope to buy another apartment because they don't like their current one.

5 ____ Xiaojing's cousin prefers to invest in the stock market because she thinks it offers better returns than the real estate market.

6 ____ Xiaojing promises to spend next Chinese New Year with her cousin's family.

F Based on the passage in (E), circle the most appropriate choice. INTERPRETIVE

1 How are Xiaojing and her cousin related?

  a Their mothers are sisters.

  b Their fathers are brothers.

  c Xiaojing's mother and her cousin's father are siblings.

2 Why does Xiaojing recommend that her cousin open a gym as an investment?

  a Both the stock market and the real estate market are sluggish.

  b She thinks that a gym would be popular and profitable.

  c There are very few gyms in Hainan.

G Look at this advertisement and answer the question in English. INTERPRETIVE

这个广告能引起你在这里买房的兴趣吗？为什么？
這個廣告能引起你在這裡買房的興趣嗎？為什麼？

_____

Imagine that you're making a deposit at a bank in China. Use this form to fill in your name, account number (012345), the amount that you are depositing (1000), the currency of the deposit (RMB), and the deposit fee (10). See if you can guess the meaning of 存期 and fill in the corresponding blank. INTERPRETIVE & PRESENTATIONAL

户　名	
账户/卡号	
种　类	
币　别	钞(汇)
存　期	起息日
存款金额：	元
手续费：	元
流水号：	
	银行签章

客户回单

戶　名	
賬戶/卡號	
種　類	
幣　別	鈔(匯)
存　期	起息日
存款金額：	元
手續費：	元
流水號：	
	銀行簽章

客戶回單

V. Writing and Grammar

A Form a character by combining the given components as indicated. Then use that character to write a word, phrase, or short sentence.

1 左边一个三点水，右边一个"紧张"的"张"，
左邊一個三點水，右邊一個"緊張"的"張"，
是 _____ 的 ____ 。

2 左边一个"火车站"的"火"，右边一个"减少"的"少"，
左邊一個"火車站"的"火"，右邊一個"減少"的"少"，
是 _____ 的 ____ 。

3 外边一个"出门"的"门"，里边一个"担心"的"心"，
外邊一個"出門"的"門"，裡邊一個"擔心"的"心"，
是 _____ 的 ____ 。

4 左边一个"禾"，右边一个刀字旁，
   左邊一個"禾"，右邊一個刀字旁，
   是 ＿＿＿＿ 的 ＿＿ 。

5 上边一个"相信"的"相"，下边一个"心事"的"心"，
   上邊一個"相信"的"相"，下邊一個"心事"的"心"，
   是 ＿＿＿＿ 的 ＿＿ 。

B Based on the images, use 合 to describe twin sisters that share everything, following the example below. PRESENTATIONAL

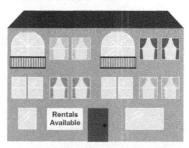

她们姐妹合租一套公寓。
她們姐妹合租一套公寓。

1

_____

2

_____

3

_____

4

_____

C Answer these questions based on the prompts. Use reduplicated verbs, following the example below. **INTERPERSONAL**

我们可以在图书馆做什么？ (read books, read newspapers, surf the Internet)
我們可以在圖書館做什麼？

→ 我们可以在图书馆看看书、看看报、上上网等等。
→ 我們可以在圖書館看看書、看看報、上上網等等。

1 我们可以上网做什么？ (send emails, download software, look up information)
我們可以上網做什麼？

_____

2 我们可以去运动中心做什么？ (play ball, do yoga)
我們可以去運動中心做什麼？

_____

3 我们可以去咖啡馆做什么？ (drink coffee, chat with friends)
我們可以去咖啡館做什麼？

_____

D Using 把, practice asking someone to complete the following tasks. PRESENTATIONAL

1 Open the window.

_____

2 Close the door.

_____

3 Finish your tea.

_____

4 Wash your cup (clean).

_____

5 Clean your room.

_____

6 Get dinner ready.

_____

E Translate these dialogues into Chinese. PRESENTATIONAL

1 Q: Which stocks have been going up lately?

_____

A: Everybody now takes environmental protection very seriously. If you don't want to flip stocks for the short term, but would like to invest over the long term (长期/長期), I think that buying stocks related to solar and wind power is not a bad idea.

_____

_____

_____

2 Person A: Did you know that there is an economist (经济学家/經濟學家) who opened a bank to provide loans to women who don't have any money, because he feels that women know how to manage and spend money?

_____

_____

_____

Person B: No, I have never heard of this economist.

_____

Person A: He also provides loans to women who don't have any money because he wants to improve women's social status. He is coming to school this evening to talk about his ideas. We can go listen together.

_____

_____

3 **Person A:** I'd like to ask some wealth-management questions—is that okay?

_____

Person B: No problem. Can I ask how old you are?

_____

Person A: Twenty-five.

_____

Person B: I think you can buy some stocks. Although the stock market sometimes goes down and it's risky to buy stocks, you're not flipping stocks over the short term, so it won't be a big problem. If you had already retired, it would be best to keep your money in the bank.

_____

_____

Person A: What about buying a house? Some people say that buying a house is also a good investment.

_____

Person B: If you are going to live in the house and don't plan on selling it, it doesn't count as an investment. It would be considered a good investment if you bought a house and rented it out.

_____

_____

Person A: Thanks. I'll go home and think about it.

_____

Translate these passages into Chinese. PRESENTATIONAL

1   My cousin (表哥) wants to buy a three-bedroom, one-living-room, and two-bathroom house, but it's outside the city and rather inconvenient to get to work. His fiancée says, "Houses in the city are too expensive. It's difficult to take out a loan. Monday through Friday, we can live with my parents or your parents. On weekends, we can bike to the suburbs (and stay there). Besides, there's bound to be a subway in the future. If we don't buy now, when housing prices go up, we won't have another opportunity."

_____

_____

_____

_____

_____

_____

_____

2   Li Wen's parents retired last month. They have been very frugal with food and other expenses for thirty years, so they have some savings in the bank. They feel that although money accumulates very slowly in the bank, it's the safest way. They don't like flipping stocks. Li Wen thinks that if you have money you should spend it. Although she has very little savings, she often flips stocks. She says houses are too expensive now. If she doesn't flip stocks and make some money, she won't have enough money to buy a house. Her parents see that she sometimes makes money and sometimes loses money. They are concerned.

_____

_____

_____

_____

_____

_____

_____

_____

G Write down your short-term and long-term financial goals. Describe how you can achieve those goals and how long it may take to reach them. When you set your goals, you should take into consideration things such as student loans, living expenses, how to be financially responsible, how to be a smart investor, what parts of life are most important to you, etc. PRESENTATIONAL

H Write a story in Chinese based on the four images below. Make sure that your story has a beginning, middle, and end, and that the transition from one picture to the next is smooth and logical. PRESENTATIONAL

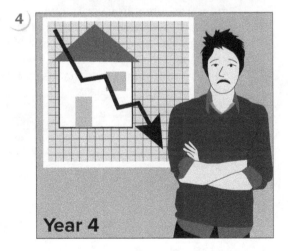

_____

_____

_____

_____

_____

中国历史
中國歷史
China's History

Check off the following language functions as you learn how to:

[ ] Narrate the general timeline of Chinese history

[ ] Describe the historical significance of major Chinese dynasties

[ ] Talk about important Chinese material and cultural artifacts

[ ] Discuss the contributions of key Chinese historical figures

As you progress through the lesson, note other language functions you would like to learn.

_____

_____

_____

Audio

A Listen to the Lesson Text audio, then mark these statements true or false. INTERPRETIVE

1 ____ Lisha and her friends will take a course in Chinese history next semester.

2 ____ Li Wen thinks very highly of Confucius' place in Chinese history.

3 ____ According to Li Wen, the First Emperor was a great and benevolent ruler.

4 ____ China had no trade with the West until the Han dynasty.

B Based on the Lesson Text audio, circle the most appropriate choice. INTERPRETIVE

1 Which dynasty is known for its poetry?
   a Qin
   b Han
   c Tang

2 Which of the following was invented during the Song dynasty?
   a gunpowder
   b movable-type printing
   c papermaking

C Listen to the Workbook Dialogue audio, then mark these statements true or false. INTERPRETIVE

1 ____ The woman seems to be more knowledgeable about Chinese history than the man.

2 ____ According to the woman, the First Emperor was the most famous emperor in Chinese history.

3 ____ According to the woman, the First Emperor did both good things and bad things.

4 ____ According to the woman, the scholars buried alive by the First Emperor had all made great contributions.

5 ____ The man seems to assume that a famous emperor must be a good emperor.

6 ____ As the woman sees it, a historical figure doesn't have to be good to warrant being famous.

D Listen to the Workbook Narrative 1 audio, then mark the statement true or false. INTERPRETIVE

1 ____ The caller is Lisha.

2 ____ Lisha's friends would like to visit the museum with her.

3 ____ The purpose of the call is to reschedule the visit to the museum.

E Based on the Workbook Narrative 2 audio, circle the most appropriate choice. INTERPRETIVE

1 The purpose of this message is to
   a ask Li Wen whether it would be okay to visit the museum the day after tomorrow.
   b inform Lisha that the day after tomorrow wouldn't be a good time to visit the museum.
   c confirm with Lisha it would be okay to visit the museum the day after tomorrow.

2 According to the caller, how does the National Museum of China compare to other world museums?
   a It is one of the largest.
   b It is one of the best.
   c It is one of the most comprehensive.

3 The caller suggests that Lisha visit the museum
   a in the afternoon and view only some of the Chinese history exhibits.
   b in the early morning and view only some of the Chinese history exhibits.
   c in the early morning and view all of the Chinese history exhibits.

4 According to the caller, what might be the reason for the increase of visitors to the museum this week?
   a expansion of the museum
   b new exhibits
   c fine weather

F _____ Listen to the Listening Rejoinder audio. After hearing the first speaker, select the best response from the four choices given by the second speaker. Indicate the letter of your choice. INTERPRETIVE

II. Pinyin and Tone

A Compare the pronunciations of the underlined characters in the two words or phrases given. Provide their initials in *pinyin*.

文<u>字</u> _____   技<u>术</u>/技<u>術</u> _____

B Compare the tones of the underlined characters in the two words or phrases given. Indicate the tones with 1 (first tone), 2 (second tone), 3 (third tone), 4 (fourth tone), or 0 (neutral tone).

<u>诗</u>人/<u>詩</u>人 _____   小<u>时</u>/小<u>時</u> _____

A Practice asking and answering these questions. INTERPERSONAL

1 孔子为什么伟大？

孔子為什麼偉大？

2 秦始皇为什么有名？

秦始皇為什麼有名？

3 唐朝在中国历史上为什么重要？

唐朝在中國歷史上為什麼重要？

B Practice speaking with these prompts. PRESENTATIONAL

1 请谈谈中国哪一个朝代给你的印象最深。

請談談中國哪一個朝代給你的印象最深。

2 你了解你的国家的历史吗？你对历史感兴趣吗？
为什么？

你了解你的國家的歷史嗎？你對歷史感興趣嗎？
為什麼？

3 Describe the typical view of the First Emperor's reign.

IV. Reading Comprehension

A Write the characters, *pinyin*, and English equivalent of each new word formed. Guess the meaning, then use a dictionary to confirm.

1 "伟大"的"伟" + "事业"的"业"

"偉大"的"偉" + "事業"的"業"

→ 伟/偉 + 业/業 → _____ _____ _____

2 "展厅"的"展" + "游览"的"览"

"展廳"的"展" + "遊覽"的"覽"

→ 展 + 览/覽 → _____ _____ _____

3 "皇帝"的"皇" + "宫殿"的"宫"

"皇帝"的"皇" + "宮殿"的"宮"

→ 皇 + 宫/宮 → _____ _____ _____

4 "修长城"的"修" + "管理"的"理"

"修長城"的"修" + "管理"的"理"

→ 修/修 + 理 → _____ _____ _____

5 "建立"的"建" + "国家"的"国"

"建立"的"建" + "國家"的"國"

→ 建 + 国/國 → _____ _____ _____

B Fill in the blanks with 参观/參觀 or 游览/遊覽. INTERPRETIVE

1 明天有大学生要来 _____ 我们的工厂，请大家做好准备。

明天有大學生要來 _____ 我們的工廠，請大家做好準備。

2 石林的石头千奇百怪，我们一边 _____，一边听导游给我们讲跟石头有关的故事。

石林的石頭千奇百怪，我們一邊 _____，一邊聽導遊給我們講跟石頭有關的故事。

3 _____ 博物馆的时候，千万别随便乱拍照。

_____ 博物館的時候，千萬別隨便亂拍照。

4 坐船从东往西 _____ 长江，感觉非常特别。

坐船從東往西 _____ 長江，感覺非常特別。

5 我们想 _____ 一下你们建筑公司在城东盖的那栋大楼，不知道方便不方便？

我們想 _____ 一下你們建築公司在城東蓋的那棟大樓，不知道方便不方便？

6 听说有个法国人坐飞机到北京 _____ 各个有名的烤鸭店。

聽說有個法國人坐飛機到北京 _____ 各個有名的烤鴨店。

C Read the passage, then mark each statement true or false. INTERPRETIVE

　　汉朝的时候中国就开始跟西方进行贸易了。因为丝绸在贸易中影响最大，所以那条商路叫"丝绸之路"。除了丝绸以外，中国人还卖给西方人很多茶。后来，中国人开始从海上跟西方进行贸易，所以又有了"海上丝绸之路"。有一些西方国家最早的茶是从丝绸之路买到的，另一些西方国家最早的茶是从海上丝绸之路买到的。很有意思的是，在这两种国家的语言里，"茶"的发音是不一样的。跟丝绸之路有关的国家，"茶"的发音和中国北方话里"茶"的发音差不多。跟海上丝绸之路有关的国家，"茶"的发音跟中国东南的一个省"茶"的发音差不多。

　　漢朝的時候中國就開始跟西方進行貿易了。因為絲綢在貿易中影響最大，所以那條商路叫"絲綢之路"。除了絲綢以外，中國人還賣給西方人很多茶。後來，中國人開始從海上跟西方進行貿易，所以又有了"海上絲綢之路"。有一些西方國家最早的茶是從絲綢之路買到的，另一些西方國家最早的茶是從海上絲綢之路買到的。很有意思的是，在這兩種國家的語言裡，"茶"的發音是不一樣的。跟絲綢之路有關的國家，"茶"的發音和中國北方話裡"茶"的發音差不多。跟海上絲綢之路有關的國家，"茶"的發音跟中國東南的一個省"茶"的發音差不多。

1 ____ The writer suggests that the Chinese started making silk during the Han dynasty.

2 ____ Despite the name "Silk Road," silk was not the only commodity in China's early trade with the West.

3 ____ Concurrent with the Silk Road, a maritime trade route between China and the West was opened.

4 ____ The writer suggests that the starting point of the Maritime Silk Road was coastal southern China.

D Based on the passage in (C), circle the most appropriate choice. INTERPRETIVE

1 According to the writer, how was tea introduced to the West?

a It was brought to the West along the Silk Road.

b It was brought to the West wrapped in silk.

c It was brought to the West along the Silk Road and the Maritime Silk Road.

2 According to the writer, differences in the pronunciation of the word "tea" among various Western languages can be ascribed to

a the different national origins of the merchants.

b preferences for different teas.

c different trade routes.

E Read the dialogue, then mark each statement true or false. INTERPRETIVE

Person A: 哎，老王，要是让你选，你最愿意做中国哪个朝代的人？

Person B: 我最愿意当唐朝人。因为唐朝的时候，中国是统一的国家，经济和人民生活都发展到比较高的水平，在很多方面都是世界最先进的。我想我不用担心找不到工作。

Person A: 我以为你是对唐诗有兴趣呢。

Person B: 我知道唐诗特别有名。我读过李白的诗，可是不太懂。

Person A: 要是你看到李白，想跟他说些什么？

Person B: 我会说："李白先生，谢谢您对中国文化的伟大贡献。"

Person A: 李白听了一定会很高兴。

Person B: 我虽然不懂李白的诗，可是我一定会成为李白的好朋友。等到我死了，我就请人把我的坟墓修在李白的坟墓旁边。

Person A: 为什么？

Person B: 这样我的坟墓就成了有名的旅游景点了。

Person A: 哎，老王，要是讓你選，你最願意做中國哪個朝代的人？

Person B: 我最願意當唐朝人。因為唐朝的時候，中國是統一的國家，經濟和人民生活都發展到比較高的水平，在很多方面都是世界最先進的。我想我不用擔心找不到工作。

Person A: 我以為你是對唐詩有興趣呢。

Person B: 我知道唐詩特別有名。我讀過李白的詩，可是不太懂。

Person A: 要是你看到李白，想跟他說些什麼？

Person B: 我會說："李白先生，謝謝您對中國文化的偉大貢獻。"

Person A: 李白聽了一定會很高興。

Person B: 我雖然不懂李白的詩，可是我一定會成為李白的好朋友。等到我死了，我就請人把我的墳墓修在李白的墳墓旁邊。

Person A: 為什麼？

Person B: 這樣我的墳墓就成了有名的旅遊景點了。

1 ____ Old Wang and his friend were born in the Tang dynasty.

2 ____ Old Wang assumes that in prosperous societies, there are plenty of job opportunities.

3 ____ Old Wang is an expert on Tang poetry.

4 ____ Old Wang thinks that Li Bai made remarkable contributions to Chinese culture.

F Based on the passage in (E), circle the most appropriate choice. INTERPRETIVE

1 Which statement most accurately describes how Old Wang would relate to Li Bai, if he had the chance?

a He would become Li Bai's friend in order to understand his poetry better.

b He would try to understand Li Bai's poetry in order to become his friend.

c Although he cannot understand Li Bai's poetry, he would become Li Bai's friend.

2 What does Old Wang say about his grave?

a He would like it to be at a famous tourist attraction.

b He believes it would become a famous tourist attraction.

c He would let Li Bai decide where his grave should be located.

G Look at this sign and follow the instruction. INTERPRETIVE

这个牌子上少了一个英文字母，是什么？请补上。

這個牌子上少了一個英文字母，是什麼？請補上。

H Look at this picture and answer the question in Chinese. INTERPERSONAL

什么东西坏了，可以来这儿修？

什麼東西壞了，可以來這兒修？

I Look at this information and answer the question in Chinese. <u>INTERPERSONAL</u>

门票是多少钱？	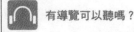 門票是多少錢？
有导览可以听吗？	有導覽可以聽嗎？
一般团体 要怎么参观？	一般團體 要怎麼參觀？
有学校团体的 参观服务吗？	有學校團體的 參觀服務嗎？
有行动不便人士 的服务措施吗？	有行動不便人士 的服務措施嗎？
有婴幼儿的 特别服务设施吗？	有嬰幼兒的 特別服務設施嗎？

什么人在什么地方会问这些问题？
什麼人在什麼地方會問這些問題？

V. Writing and Grammar

A Form a character by combining the given components as indicated. Then use that character to write a word, phrase, or short sentence.

1 上边一个"白色"的"白"，下边一个"王"，
  上邊一個"白色"的"白"，下邊一個"王"，
  是 ＿＿＿＿＿＿＿ 的 ＿＿＿＿ 。

2 左边一个"女性"的"女"，右边一个"台北"的"台"，
  左邊一個"女性"的"女"，右邊一個"台北"的"台"，
  是 ＿＿＿＿＿＿＿ 的 ＿＿＿＿ 。

3 上边一个"朝代"的"代"，下边一个"衣服"的"衣"，

上邊一個"朝代"的"代"，下邊一個"衣服"的"衣"，

是 ＿＿＿＿＿＿ 的 ＿＿＿ 。

4 上边一个"工作"的"工"，下边一个"贝"，

上邊一個"工作"的"工"，下邊一個"貝"，

是 ＿＿＿＿＿＿ 的 ＿＿＿ 。

5 左边一个"纟"，右边一个"补充"的"充"，

左邊一個"糸"，右邊一個"補充"的"充"，

是 ＿＿＿＿＿＿ 的 ＿＿＿ 。

B First, draw a line connecting each person with the title he/she is associated with. Then, use 之一 to describe each person's status in the world, following the example below. INTERPRETIVE & PRESENTATIONAL

孔子　　　　　教育家

→ 孔子是世界上最伟大的教育家之一。

→ 孔子是世界上最偉大的教育家之一。

1	Aristotle	a	哲学家/哲學家
2	Thomas Edison	b	画家/畫家
3	Marie Curie	c	文学家/文學家
4	Shakespeare	d	发明家/發明家
5	Frida Kahlo	e	科学家/科學家

1 ＿＿＿＿＿＿＿＿＿＿＿＿＿＿＿＿＿＿＿＿＿＿＿＿＿＿＿＿＿

2 ＿＿＿＿＿＿＿＿＿＿＿＿＿＿＿＿＿＿＿＿＿＿＿＿＿＿＿＿＿

3 ＿＿＿＿＿＿＿＿＿＿＿＿＿＿＿＿＿＿＿＿＿＿＿＿＿＿＿＿＿

4 ＿＿＿＿＿＿＿＿＿＿＿＿＿＿＿＿＿＿＿＿＿＿＿＿＿＿＿＿＿

5 ＿＿＿＿＿＿＿＿＿＿＿＿＿＿＿＿＿＿＿＿＿＿＿＿＿＿＿＿＿

C Based on the prompts, conduct online research on Beijing, Shanghai, Tokyo, and New York. Then complete the sentences using 其中, following the example below. PRESENTATIONAL

population

北京、上海、东京、纽约都是世界上的大城市，其中上海的人口最多。

北京、上海、東京、紐約都是世界上的大城市，其中上海的人口最多。

1 land area

北京、上海、东京、纽约都是世界上的大城市，

北京、上海、東京、紐約都是世界上的大城市，

_____

2 number of subway lines

北京、上海、东京、纽约都是世界上的大城市，

北京、上海、東京、紐約都是世界上的大城市，

_____

3 cost of housing

北京、上海、东京、纽约都是世界上的大城市，

北京、上海、東京、紐約都是世界上的大城市，

_____

4 air pollution

北京、上海、东京、纽约都是世界上的大城市，

北京、上海、東京、紐約都是世界上的大城市，

_____

D Draw a line connecting each IC character with the topic he/she knows more about than his/her friends. Then use 在⋯方面 to state that fact in a sentence, following the example below. INTERPRETIVE & PRESENTATIONAL

自助游/自助遊

→ 在自助游方面，柯林比其他人都懂得多。

→ 在自助遊方面，柯林比其他人都懂得多。

1    a 中国历史/中國歷史

2    b 电脑网络/電腦網絡

3    c 健身与饮食/健身與飲食

4    d 环保与节能/環保與節能

1 _____

2 _____

3 _____

4 _____

E Based on your own circumstances, use 跟⋯有关（系）/跟⋯有關（係） to answer these questions, following the example below. INTERPERSONAL

Person A: 你比较喜欢看哪方面的书？政治、经济、文化，还是历史？

你比較喜歡看哪方面的書？政治、經濟、文化，還是歷史？

Person B: 我比较喜欢看跟文化有关的书。

我比較喜歡看跟文化有關的書。

1 你常常上网查哪方面的资料？股市、房价、购物、旅游，还是天气？

你常常上網查哪方面的資料？股市、房價、購物、旅遊，還是天氣？

---

2 你比较注意哪方面的新闻？政治、经济、社会，还是国际？

你比較注意哪方面的新聞？政治、經濟、社會，還是國際？

---

3 哪方面的事情更会引起你的重视？健身、环保、节能，还是理财？

哪方面的事情更會引起你的重視？健身、環保、節能，還是理財？

F Based on the images, use 再也不 to state each character's New Year's resolution, following the example below. PRESENTATIONAL

柯林说从明年开始他再也不喝瓶装水了。
柯林說從明年開始他再也不喝瓶裝水了。

1

2

_____

3

_____

G Translate these dialogues into Chinese. PRESENTATIONAL

1 **Teacher:** Tomorrow we'll have a test on Chinese history. Please go over the emperors of the Qing dynasty this evening.

_____

_____

Student: Teacher, we don't like tests or reviewing.

_____

_____

Teacher: Everybody knows that Confucius left us a lot of sayings. Among those, "Having friends from afar—isn't that a great joy!" is one of the most famous. There's another saying that is equally famous. That is, "Studying and reviewing frequently—isn't that a great pleasure (学而时习之，不亦乐乎/學而時習之，不亦樂乎)!" Everyone, happy reviewing this evening.

_____

_____

_____

_____

2 **Person A:** Have you visited the Terracotta Warrior Museum?

_____

Person B: No, but I'd like to. I'm very interested in the First Emperor of the Qin dynasty.

_____

Person A: The First Emperor is important in Chinese history, but many people don't like him because he killed many scholars. He also made many people build palaces and a tomb for him.

_____

_____

Person B: Whether you like him or not, I think he was very influential in Chinese history. For example, he unified the Chinese script.

_____

_____

Person A: I agree with that. The Qin dynasty had a great impact on the Han dynasty's political and economic development.

_____

_____

3 **Person A:** Let's go climb the Great Wall tomorrow. How about it?

_____

Person B: Great. I've wanted to go for a long time, but I've never had the opportunity. I hear that the Great Wall has a history of about two or three thousand years. Construction of the Great Wall started before the Qin dynasty.

_____

_____

_____

Person A: That's right, but our history teacher says that the Great Wall that we see today was mostly built during the Ming dynasty (明朝).

_____

_____

_____

Person B: How do we get there?

_____

Person A: We can take the bus.

_____

Person B: It's boring to take the bus. Let's bike there, shall we?

_____

Person A: OK. It's a deal! Biking not only saves money, it's also good for health.

_____

H Translate this passage into Chinese. PRESENTATIONAL

Confucius said, "Having friends visiting from afar—isn't that a great joy!" Welcome to Shandong (山东/山東), everyone. Confucius is the most important educator and thinker in Chinese history and had a great impact on China. Shandong is the birthplace of Confucius. The most famous Temple of Confucius is right in Shandong. There are also many tourist sights in Shandong—for instance, Mt. Tai (泰山). I hope that besides having lots of opportunities to practice Chinese in Shandong, everyone will also be able to climb Mt. Tai. Finally, I'd like to give these T-shirts printed (印) with Confucius' words to everyone as a gift.

_____

_____

_____

_____

_____

_____

_____

_____

_____

_____

I Write a story in Chinese based on the four images below. Make sure that your story has a beginning, middle, and end, and that the transition from one picture to the next is smooth and logical. PRESENTATIONAL

1)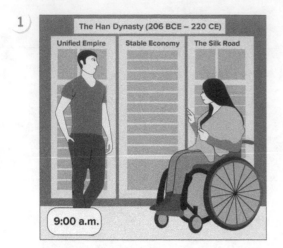

2)

3)

The Qing Dynasty (1644 – 1911)

Underdeveloped Science and Technology | Unstable Politics and Economy | The 1911 Revolution

10:00 a.m.

4)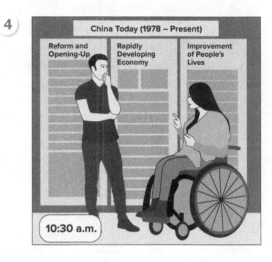

_____

_____

_____

_____

_____

_____

_____

_____

_____

_____

面试
面試
Job Interview

 Check off the following language functions as you learn how to:

[ ] Explain why China has been able to attract talent and corporations from overseas

[ ] Describe overseas returnees and their nicknames

[ ] Recount a nerve-racking interview

[ ] Handle typical job interview questions

As you progress through the lesson, note other language functions you would like to learn.

_____

_____

_____

Audio

A Listen to the Lesson Text audio, then mark each statement true or false. INTERPRETIVE

1 _____ People who return from overseas are sometimes playfully called "sea turtles," because the word for "sea turtle" sounds the same as the word for "returnee from overseas."

2 _____ Since it was her first job interview, Lin Xuemei was initially nervous.

3 _____ Xuemei said that she wanted to work in Beijing in order to be with her boyfriend.

B Based on the Lesson Text audio, circle the most appropriate choice. INTERPRETIVE

1 What did Xuemei show the general manager to convince him that she had not returned to China due to her lack of success in America?

a recommendation letters from her professors

b offer letters from two American companies

c her university transcript

2 According to Xuemei, what's her biggest weakness?

a She tends to get nervous under pressure.

b She loves snacks too much.

c She does not know how to get enough rest.

3 Why is Xuemei optimistic about her job interview?

a The general manager told her to wait for good news.

b She was able to demonstrate her familiarity with the company's products.

c Similar companies in the U.S. wanted to hire her.

C Listen to the Workbook Dialogue audio, then mark these statements true or false. INTERPRETIVE

1 _____ According to the woman, the Chinese automotive industry started about twenty years ago.

2 _____ The Dadi Company builds cars that produce less pollution.

3 _____ The man is looking for a job in the automotive industry.

4 _____ The man believes that the woman's company offers higher compensation than its competitors.

5 _____ The man likes the woman's company because it is profitable.

6 _____ In the end, the woman realizes that the man is a true environmentalist.

D | Listen to the Workbook Narrative 1 audio, then mark these statements true or false. INTERPRETIVE

1 ____ Before she started applying for jobs, the speaker was a student.

2 ____ The speaker did not receive offers from two of the companies that she interviewed at.

3 ____ The speaker did not like the companies that had extended her offers.

4 ____ The speaker will probably start her new job next week.

E | Based on the Workbook Narrative 2 audio, circle the most appropriate choice. INTERPRETIVE

1 The speaker is
   a one of Miss Zhang's professional references.
   b the CEO of a Japanese company.
   c the head of a Chinese company.

2 The speaker argues in favor of
   a hiring Miss Zhang.
   b increased collaboration with Japanese companies.
   c new marketing efforts in Japan.

3 Which of the following does the speaker not mention as one of Miss Zhang's credentials?
   a She was a good college student.
   b She has work experience in Japan.
   c She majored in a field that is closely related to the speaker's company's business.

4 How did Miss Zhang become familiar with the products and market of the speaker's company?
   a She did research about the company on the Internet.
   b Her previous company collaborated with the speaker's company.
   c She learned about the company from her conversation with the speaker.

F | ____ Listen to the Workbook Listening Rejoinder audio. After hearing the first speaker, select the best response from the four choices given by the second speaker. Indicate the letter of your choice. INTERPRETIVE

II. Pinyin and Tone

A | Compare the pronunciations of the underlined characters in the two words or phrases given. Provide their initials in *pinyin*.

吸引 _____

上衣湿了/上衣濕了 _____

B Compare the tones of the underlined characters in the two words or phrases given. Indicate the tones with 1 (first tone), 2 (second tone), 3 (third tone), 4 (fourth tone), or 0 (neutral tone).

<u>答</u>应/<u>答</u>應 _____   回<u>答</u> _____

╔══════════════════════════╗
║   **III. Speaking**   ║
╚══════════════════════════╝

A Practice asking and answering these questions. INTERPERSONAL

1 什么样的人被叫做"海龟"?
   什麼樣的人被叫做"海龜"?

2 为什么中国吸引很多的跨国公司和人材?
   為什麼中國吸引很多的跨國公司和人材?

3 请谈谈让你紧张的一次面试。
   請談談讓你緊張的一次面試。

B Practice speaking with these prompts. PRESENTATIONAL

1 请谈谈怎么样安排时间才能有益于学习或工作。
   請談談怎麼樣安排時間才能有益於學習或工作。

2 请谈谈你自己的优点与缺点。
   請談談你自己的優點與缺點。

3 Xuemei impressed the general manager during her interview. If you had been in Xuemei's place, how do you think you would have done? Explain whether and why you would handle the interview in a similar or different way.

A Write the characters, *pinyin*, and English equivalent of each new word formed. Guess the meaning, then use a dictionary to confirm.

1 "西方"的"西" + "服装"的"装"

"西方"的"西" + "服裝"的"裝"

→ 西 + 装/裝 → _____ _____ _____

2 "湿" + "温度"的"度"

"濕" + "溫度"的"度"

→ 湿/濕 + 度 → _____ _____ _____

3 "严肃"的"肃" + "安静"的"静"

"嚴肅"的"肅" + "安靜"的"靜"

→ 肃/肅 + 静/靜 → _____ _____ _____

4 "阴转多云"的"阴" + "太阳"的"阳"

"陰轉多雲"的"陰" + "太陽"的"陽"

→ 阴/陰 + 阳/陽 → _____ _____ _____

5 "解释"的"解" + "回答"的"答"

"解釋"的"解" + "回答"的"答"

→ 解/解 + 答 → _____ _____ _____

B Read the passage, then mark the statements true or false. INTERPRETIVE

　　对从西方国家大学毕业的中国留学生来说，回中国好还是留在西方好，这是一个引起很多人思考的问题。不少中国留学生觉得，回中国找工作不是一个很容易的决定。为什么呢？因为中国的公司文化跟西方不完全一样，他们担心可能不太适应。还有，中国的环保是一个大问题，一些大城市的空气质量不好，雾霾严重。可是另外一些中国留学生认为现在是回中国工作的好机会。为什么呢？因为中国的经济发展很快，很多中国公司需要人材。中国留学生学习了西方的管理办法，又懂中国的风俗习惯，所以一定会很受欢迎。我觉得这两种看法都有道理。不过从西方回中国的"海龟"一定会越来越多，中国的环境也开始变好了。

　　對從西方國家大學畢業的中國留學生來說，回中國好還是留在西方好，這是一個引起很多人思考的問題。不少中國留學生覺得，回中國找工作不是一個很容易的決定。為什麼呢？因為中國的公司文化跟西方不完全一樣，他們擔心可能不太適應。還有，中國的環保是一個大問題，一些大城市的空氣質量不好，霧霾嚴重。可是另外一些中國留學生認為現在是回中國工作的好機會。為什麼呢？因為中國的經濟發展很快，很多中國公司需要人材。中國留學生學習了西方的管理辦法，又懂中國的風俗習慣，所以一定會很受歡迎。我覺得這兩種看法都有道理。不過從西方回中國的"海龜"一定會越來越多，中國的環境也開始變好了。

1 ____ The writer does not lean toward either of the views presented.

2 ____ According to the passage, most Chinese students in Western countries return to China after receiving their degrees.

3 ____ The writer predicts that the number of Chinese students returning to China will increase.

C Based on the passage in (B), circle the most appropriate choice. INTERPRETIVE

1 What factors play into some Chinese students' decision not to return to China?

    a higher pay and better management in Western companies

    b different corporate culture in Chinese companies and bad air pollution in some Chinese cities

    c environmental issues and a lack of high-level jobs in Chinese companies

2 Why do some Chinese students think that now is the best time for them to return to China?

    a They are needed by Chinese companies.

    b The rate of economic development in China is high.

    c China will see a decrease in environmental pollution.

3 What do some Chinese students think would enhance their job prospects in China?

    a their foreign-language ability and knowledge of Western corporate culture

    b their familiarity with both Western and Chinese culture

    c their knowledge of Western corporate culture and familiarity with Chinese culture

D   Read the passage, then mark the statements true or false. INTERPRETIVE

柯林的日记

今天是不平常的一天。下午四点，我刚下课，雪梅就给我发来微信，说她收到录用通知了。我们太高兴了，晚上我们一起去一家西餐馆儿吃了一顿，为她的事业成功干杯。回宿舍以后，我想了很多。我知道雪梅很喜欢那家跨国公司，她去那儿工作不是短期打算。我很相信雪梅的能力，她在那儿一定会发展得很好。看起来，她明年回美国是不太可能了。为了和雪梅在一起，我也必须考虑在北京找工作了。我的中文虽然最近进步不小，可是要在跨国企业里工作，可能还不够好，特别是听力和英翻中；但是我也有优点，那就是我大学的专业是国际贸易，而且有实习经验。我相信我也能找到一个适合我的工作。可是长期在中国生活，我会习惯吗？有空的时候我要找马克好好儿聊聊。他在北京生活了好几年了，一定能给我一些好的建议。

柯林的日記

今天是不平常的一天。下午四點，我剛下課，雪梅就給我發來微信，說她收到錄用通知了。我們太高興了，晚上我們一起去一家西餐館兒吃了一頓，為她的事業成功乾杯。回宿舍以後，我想了很多。我知道雪梅很喜歡那家跨國公司，她去那兒工作不是短期打算。我很相信雪梅的能力，她在那兒一定會發展得很好。看起來，她明年回美國是不太可能了。為了和雪梅在一起，我也必須考慮在北京找工作了。我的中文雖然最近進步不小，可是要在跨國企業裡工作，可能還不夠好，特別是聽力和英翻中；但是我也有優點，那就是我大學的專業是國際貿易，而且有實習經驗。我相信我也能找到一個適合我的工作。可是長期在中國生活，我會習慣嗎？有空的時候我要找馬克好好兒聊聊。他在北京生活了好幾年了，一定能給我一些好的建議。

1 ____ The company notified Xuemei via text message that she was hired.

2 ____ Ke Lin and Xuemei ate at a Western-style restaurant yesterday evening.

3 ____ Ke Lin plans to return with Xuemei to the U.S. next year.

4 ____ Ke Lin is completely confident in his Chinese language skills.

E Based on the passage in (D), circle the most appropriate choice. INTERPRETIVE

1 What does Ke Lin predict regarding Xuemei's career at the company?

  a She will have a long and successful career there.

  b After being successful there, she will return to the U.S. next year.

  c She will have great success there, and join Ke Lin at a different company later.

2 Why does Ke Lin start thinking about finding a job in Beijing?

  a to improve his Chinese

  b to put his knowledge of international trade to practice

  c to be with Xuemei

3 How does Ke Lin feel about being in Beijing for a long time?

  a He is confident about his chances of finding a job, but unsure about adapting to living in Beijing over the long term.

  b He is confident about his chances of finding a job and about adapting to living in Beijing over the long term.

  c He is unsure about his chances of finding a job and about adapting to living in Beijing over the long term.

F Look at this advertisement and answer the question in Chinese. INTERPERSONAL

这份工作什么时候上班薪水最高?

這份工作什麼時候上班薪水最高?

_____

G Fill in the blanks with 常常 or 往往. INTERPRETIVE

1 经理告诉雪梅开始上班以后 _____ 需要出国开会。

经理告诉雪梅开始上班以后 _____ 需要出国开会。

經理告訴雪梅開始上班以後 _____ 需要出國開會。

2 太极拳要打得好必须 _____ 练习。

太極拳要打得好必須 _____ 練習。

3 我很喜欢参观博物馆,无论去哪个博物馆, _____ 都得花好几个小时的时间。

我很喜歡參觀博物館,無論去哪個博物館, _____ 都得花好幾個小時的時間。

4 刚从大学毕业的人,如果没有实习经验, _____ 很难找到工作。

剛從大學畢業的人,如果沒有實習經驗, _____ 很難找到工作。

5 面试雪梅的人 _____ 很严肃,一点儿都不幽默,甚至有点儿吓人。

面試雪梅的人 _____ 很嚴肅,一點兒都不幽默,甚至有點兒嚇人。

Look at this photo and respond to the prompt. **INTERPRETIVE**

请把这个天气预报翻译成英文。
請把這個天氣預報翻譯成英文。

_____

I Read this survey form and answer the questions that follow. **INTERPRETIVE**

顾客意见调查表	顧客意見調查表
您是否第一次在这里消费？ □ 是　　　□ 不是	您是否第一次在這裡消費？ □ 是　　　□ 不是
服务生是否亲切地欢迎您？ □ 是　　　□ 不是	服務生是否親切地歡迎您？ □ 是　　　□ 不是
服务生是否主动向您推荐饮料或餐点？ □ 是　　　□ 不是	服務生是否主動向您推薦飲料或餐點？ □ 是　　　□ 不是
服务生是否主动询问您对我们的服务是否满意？ □ 是　　　□ 不是	服務生是否主動詢問您對我們的服務是否滿意？ □ 是　　　□ 不是
服务生是否主动向您推荐饮料续杯？ □ 是　　　□ 不是	服務生是否主動向您推薦飲料續杯？ □ 是　　　□ 不是
您对服务生所提供服务的满意程度？ □ 很满意　□ 满意　□ 一般　□ 不满意	您對服務生所提供服務的滿意程度？ □ 很滿意　□ 滿意　□ 一般　□ 不滿意
您对整体餐饮品质的满意程度？ □ 很满意　□ 满意　□ 一般　□ 不满意	您對整體餐飲品質的滿意程度？ □ 很滿意　□ 滿意　□ 一般　□ 不滿意

1 Who do you think is conducting the survey and who is being surveyed?

_____

2 What is the Chinese colloquial equivalent of 是否 in this context?

_____

3 Think back to your last experience in a similar setting. If you were given this survey, which questions would you choose to answer?

_____

> ## V. Writing and Grammar

A Form a character by combining the given components as indicated. Then use that character to write a word, phrase, or short sentence.

1 左边一个口，右边一个"来不及"的"及"，

左邊一個口，右邊一個"來不及"的"及"，

是 _____ 的 _____ 。

2 左边一个三点水，右边一个"每天"的"每"，

左邊一個三點水，右邊一個"每天"的"每"，

是 _____ 的 _____ 。

3 上边一个"隹"，下边一个"口"，

上邊一個"隹"，下邊一個"口"，

是 _____ 的 _____ 。

4 左边一个"车"，右边一个"专业"的"专"，

左邊一個"車"，右邊一個"專業"的"專"，

是 _____ 的 _____ 。

5 左边一个提手旁，右边一个"屋子"的"屋"，

左邊一個提手旁，右邊一個"屋子"的"屋"，

是 _____ 的 _____ 。

B First, draw a line connecting each of the full forms on the left with an abbreviation on the right. Then, use 叫做 to state how they relate and translate the Chinese term into English, following the example below. INTERPRETIVE & PRESENTATIONAL

海外归来／海外歸來　　海归／海歸

→ "海外归来"也叫做"海归"，英文翻译成 "returning from overseas"

→ "海外歸來"也叫做"海歸"，英文翻譯成 "returning from overseas"

1　国际贸易／國際貿易　　　　a　国企／國企

2　环境保护／環境保護　　　　b　国贸／國貿

3　节约能源／節約能源　　　　c　电邮／電郵

4　国有企业／國有企業　　　　d　丝路／絲路

5　科学技术／科學技術　　　　e　节能／節能

6　电子邮件／電子郵件　　　　f　科技

7　丝绸之路／絲綢之路　　　　g　环保／環保

1 _____

2 _____

3 _____

4 _____

5 _____

6 _____

7 _____

C Based on commonsense knowledge and the prompts, state an ideal circumstance by using 越⋯⋯越⋯⋯, following the example below. PRESENTATIONAL

rent

房租越便宜越好。

房租越便宜越好。

1 Sichuanese cuisine

_____

2 salary

_____

3 pressure at work

_____

4 air (to breathe)

_____

5 bank interest

_____

D Complete these exchanges using 既然, following the example below. INTERPERSONAL

Person A: 你自己去看电影吧，我累了，想回家。

你自己去看電影吧，我累了，想回家。

Person B: 既然你想回家，我也回家吧。

既然你想回家，我也回家吧。

1 Person A: 我想投资股市，可是我没钱。

我想投資股市，可是我沒錢。

Person B: _____，干吗投资股市？

_____，幹嗎投資股市？

2 Person A: 我想搬到城里去住，但城里空气污染挺严重的。

我想搬到城裡去住，但城裡空氣汙染挺嚴重的。

Person B: _____, 就別搬了吧！

_____, 就別搬了吧！

3 Person A: 刚才那位张先生面试的表现，我很满意。

剛才那位張先生面試的表現，我很滿意。

Person B: _____, 就通知他下星期来上班。

_____, 就通知他下星期來上班。

E | Complete these exchanges, using 好在 to introduce good decisions made by you or your family. Follow the example below. PRESENTATIONAL

Person A: 最近世界上很多国家有能源危机。 (solar power)

最近世界上很多國家有能源危機。

Person B: 好在我们用太阳能发电。

好在我們用太陽能發電。

1 Person A: 最近很多人炒股赔了很多钱。 (money in the bank)

最近很多人炒股賠了很多錢。

Person B: _____

2 Person A: 医生说熬夜对身体不好。 (never do it)

醫生說熬夜對身體不好。

Person B: _____

3 Person A: 科学家说少吃肉，多吃青菜、水果有益于身体健康。 (vegetarian)

科學家說少吃肉，多吃青菜、水果有益於身體健康。

Person B: _____

F Complete the following sentences using the "Verb 着 verb 着 /Verb 著 verb 著" pattern, following the example below. PRESENTATIONAL

天明看电视，看着看着就睡着了。
天明看電視，看著看著就睡著了。

1

马克爬山，_____。
馬克爬山，_____。

2

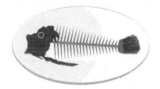

柯林吃鱼，_____。
柯林吃魚，_____。

3

丽莎听故事，_____。
麗莎聽故事，_____。

First, draw a line connecting each of the characters on the left with an area of expertise on the right. Then, form a sentence describing each match, following the example below. INTERPRETIVE & PRESENTATIONAL

林雪梅的舅妈   投资

林雪梅的舅媽   投資

→ 林雪梅的舅妈善于投资，是投资方面的人材。

→ 林雪梅的舅媽善於投資，是投資方面的人材。

1	林雪梅	a	网络设计/網絡設計
2	总经理/總經理	b	理财/理財
3	张天明/張天明	c	销售/銷售
4	天明的表哥	d	管理

1 _____

2 _____

3 _____

4 _____

H   Translate these dialogues into Chinese. PRESENTATIONAL

1   **Person A:**   What are you looking for on the Internet?

_____

     Person B: I'm looking for job information.

_____

     Person A: What area do you want to work in?

_____

     Person B: I'd like to find something to do with environmental protection. I'm very interested in this solar-energy company.

_____

Person A: Is that a multinational company? You are not only good at researching and developing new technologies, but you also understand Chinese and Western culture. They will definitely welcome a "sea turtle" like you.

_____

_____

_____

2 **Person A:** Can you tell me why you want to apply for this job?

_____

Person B: I majored in environmental studies in college. In addition, solar energy doesn't pollute the environment. It's good for protecting the environment.

_____

_____

Person A: Do you have work experience?

_____

Person B: I interned at an American solar-energy company for six months.

_____

Person A: Do you plan to work in China on a short-term basis?

_____

Person B: No, I was born and grew up in China, and my parents are in China. That's why I plan to work in China over the long term (长期/長期).

_____

_____

Person A: Great. Please wait for our notification.

_____

3 **Person A:** What do you think of the person who came for the interview today?

_____

Person B: I think she is great; she has many strengths. Both her Chinese and English are good. Furthermore, she has internship experience in the United States.

_____

Person A: But she has one shortcoming. She doesn't have any experience in international sales.

_____

Person B: She just graduated from college, so it would be unlikely for her to have a lot of experience in sales. From the way she answered the questions, she seemed very intelligent. Besides, her major in college was environmental studies. I believe that she has the ability to present (introduce) our products clearly to our customers (客户).

_____

_____

_____

_____

Person A: That makes sense. Let's hire her.

_____

4 **Person A:** Tomorrow you'll start working at the company. You must arrange your time scientifically. Besides working, you have to pay attention to rest. Don't stay up late. Learn from others' strengths.

_____

_____

Person A: Mom, don't worry. I know. I'm not a little kid anymore.

_____

Person B: Since you know, I won't say it any more. Otherwise, the more I say, the more unhappy you'll be.

_____

_____

I Translate these passages into Chinese.

1   We are a multinational, "green" beverage company. Currently, we need a sales manager. Applicants (申请者/申請者) must be good at sales and speak good Chinese and English. Those who have overseas sales experience and understand technology are even better. At our company, there is gender equality and equal pay for equal work.

_____

_____

_____

_____

_____

2   My interview today went smoothly. The manager asked me to talk about the good and bad aspects of their products. Luckily, I had prepared well, and the more I explained, the more pleased the manager was. Before I went into his office, everyone told me the manager was stern, but as long as you correctly answered his questions, he would not be that scary.

_____

_____

_____

_____

_____

J It's important to know yourself well before you can plan your career. Write a paragraph assessing your personality, education, interests, preferences, expertise, strengths, and weaknesses. Then, conclude with what type of job may be a good fit for you.

K Write a story in Chinese based on the four images below. Make sure that your story has a beginning, middle, and end, and that the transition from one picture to the next is smooth and logical. PRESENTATIONAL

世界变小了
世界變小了
The World Is Getting Smaller

✔ Check off the following language functions as you learn how to:

[ ] Explain the purpose of a gathering

[ ] Request and otter help

[ ] Discuss adjusting to life in a new country

[ ] Describe how the world is getting smaller

As you progress through the lesson, note other language functions you would like to learn.

_____

_____

_____

Audio

A Listen to the Lesson Text audio, then circle the most appropriate choice. INTERPRETIVE

1 **Xuemei and Ke Lin are throwing a party to**

   a celebrate Xuemei's new job.

   b welcome Li Zhe and send off Zhang Tianming and Lisha.

   c both of the above

2 **On Xuemei's first business trip for her new job, she will**

   a go to Europe to study the latest solar technology.

   b go to Europe to market solar panels and energy-efficient batteries.

   c go to America to market solar panels and energy-efficient batteries.

3 **How does Li Zhe know the general manager of the company that hired Xuemei?**

   a The general manager is a friend of Li Zhe's brother.

   b The general manager is a friend of Xuemei's uncle.

   c The general manager once wrote a letter of recommendation for Xuemei.

4 **Which job has Mark not had in China?**

   a actor

   b salesman

   c language teacher

5 **What does Lisha cite as the main reason for her easy adjustment to life in Beijing?**

   a help from Tianming

   b help from her Chinese professors

   c help from Li Wen and her family

6 **After talking to people at the party, Li Zhe becomes**

   a more confident about his life in Beijing.

   b prouder of his brother's friend.

   c excited about his internship.

B Listen to the Workbook Dialogue audio, then mark each statement true or false. INTERPRETIVE

1 ____ The woman is the general manager of the company.

2 ____ Li Zhe will work in the sales department for three months and then be transferred to another department.

3 ____ The general manager will discuss Li Zhe's work with Lin Xuemei.

4 ____ Lin Xuemei will be Li Zhe's supervisor.

5 ____ The woman already knew that Li Zhe and Lin Xuemei had attended the same university in the U.S.

Listen to the Workbook Narrative 1 audio, then circle the most appropriate choice. INTERPRETIVE

1 **Who is Zhang Hong?**
  a   an international student from China
  b   an employee at a company in Shanghai
  c   a professor in Beijing

2 **Why is Li Xin leaving soon?**
  a   She is going to study in Beijing.
  b   She is going to take a job in Shanghai.
  c   She is going to teach in Tianjin.

3 **Who will they be welcoming at the gathering?**
  a   two students from Beijing
  b   two students from Shanghai
  c   two students from Tianjin

D Listen to the Workbook Narrative 2 audio, then mark each statement true or false. INTERPRETIVE

1 ____   The speaker is a new student from Beijing.

2 ____   The speaker is sad that Li Xin won't be at the party.

3 ____   The speaker called Little Wang because they hadn't seen each other in a while.

E ____ Listen to the Workbook Listening Rejoinder audio. After hearing the first speaker, select the best response from the four choices given by the second speaker. Indicate the letter of your choice. INTERPRETIVE

II. Pinyin and Tone

A Compare the pronunciations of the underlined characters in the two words or phrases given. Provide their initials in *pinyin*.

聚会／聚會 _____   庆祝／慶祝 _____

B Compare the pronunciation and tones of the underlined characters in the two words or phrases given. Write them out in *pinyin* and indicate the tones with 1 (first tone), 2 (second tone), 3 (third tone), 4 (fourth tone), 0 (neutral tone), or tone marks.

差不多／差不多 _____   出差／出差 _____

A Practice asking and answering these questions. INTERPRETIVE

1 在一个为人接风的聚会上，说些什么话比较合适？

在一個為人接風的聚會上，說些什麼話比較合適？

2 在一个给人饯行的聚会上，说些什么话比较合适？

在一個給人餞行的聚會上，說些什麼話比較合適？

3 如果你去中国，你觉得你能不能很快地适应那儿的
生活？请解释。

如果你去中國，你覺得你能不能很快地適應那兒的
生活？請解釋。

B Practice speaking with these prompts. PRESENTATIONAL

1 请谈谈去国外留学或生活有什么好处。

請談談去國外留學或生活有什麼好處。

2 请谈谈在国外留学或生活应该注意些什么。

請談談在國外留學或生活應該注意些什麼。

3 Predict how you would adapt to life in China. Would the food, weather, air quality, social life,
study habits, or work routine take you the longest to get used to?

IV. Reading Comprehension

A Write the characters, *pinyin*, and English equivalent of each new word formed. Guess the meaning,
then use a dictionary to confirm.

1 "聚会"的"聚" + "晚餐"的"餐"

"聚會"的"聚" + "晚餐"的"餐"

→ 聚/聚 + 餐 → _____ _____ _____

2 "庆祝"的"庆" + "成功"的"功"

"慶祝"的"慶" + "成功"的"功"

→ 庆/慶 + 功 → _____ _____ _____

3 "关照"的"关" + "放心"的"心"

"關照"的"關" + "放心"的"心"

→ 关/關 + 心 → _____ _____ _____

4 "电视剧"的"剧" + "一本书"的"本"

"電視劇"的"劇" + "一本書"的"本"

→ 剧/劇 + 本 → _____ _____ _____

5 "联系"的"联" + "网络"的"络"

"聯繫"的"聯" + "網絡"的"絡"

→ 联/聯 + 络/絡 → _____ _____ _____

B 者, 员/員, and 家 can all refer to people. Study these words and write down their English equivalents. INTERPRETIVE

1 者

　　a 读者/讀者　　　　_____

　　b 作者　　　　　　_____

　　c 老者　　　　　　_____

　　d 教育工作者　　　_____

　　e 学者/學者　　　_____

2 员/員

　　a 服务员/服務員　　_____

　　b 售货员/售貨員　　_____

　　c 运动员/運動員　　_____

　　d 队员/隊員　　　　_____

　　e 演员/演員　　　　_____

3 家

　　a 哲学家/哲學家　　　_____

　　b 科学家/科學家　　　_____

　　c 经济学家/經濟學家　　_____

　　d 发明家/發明家　　　_____

　　e 教育家　　　　　　_____

　　f 思想家　　　　　　_____

C Fill in the blanks with the appropriate verbs.

　　换　　　　用　　　　没有/沒有　　　充电/充電 (chōng diàn)

　　　　　　　　　　　　　　　　　　　　　　(to fill with electricity, to charge)

1 电脑的电池 _____ 电了，需要 _____ 。

　　電腦的電池 _____ 電了，需要 _____ 。

2 我没有 _____ 过汽车电池，你呢?

　　我沒有 _____ 過汽車電池，你呢?

3 你的手机电池可以 _____ 多久?

　　你的手機電池可以 _____ 多久?

D Read the passage, then mark the statements true or false. INTERPRETIVE

　　　　上个星期我在一家超市看到一位年轻的西方人，觉得很面熟，一想，原来就是刚看过的电视剧里的演员! 我跟他聊了几句，很快地成了朋友。他是法国人，前年冬天来中国的，所以中文名字叫冬华。冬华来中国是为了学中文，周末也当法文家教。他教七八个学生，其中有个孩子的父亲是个挺有名的演员。有一次那个孩子的父亲正在拍一个电视剧，剧里边有位年轻的外国律师，找不到合适的人演，他想到了冬华，就介绍他去试试。冬华一开始很紧张，可是很快就适应了，大家都对他很满意。后来，冬华又在另外两个电视剧里出现过，成了一位演员。

　　上個星期我在一家超市看到一位年輕的西方人，覺得很面熟，一想，原來就是剛看過的電視劇裡的演員！我跟他聊了幾句，很快地成了朋友。他是法國人，前年冬天來中國的，所以中文名字叫冬華。冬華來中國是為了學中文，週末也當法文家教。他教七八個學生，其中有個孩子的父親是個挺有名的演員。有一次那個孩子的父親正在拍一個電視劇，劇裡邊有位年輕的外國律師，找不到合適的人演，他想到了冬華，就介紹他去試試。冬華一開始很緊張，可是很快就適應了，大家都對他很滿意。後來，冬華又在另外兩個電視劇裡出現過，成了一位演員。

1 ____ The writer is an actor.

2 ____ Dong Hua received his Chinese name from his Chinese teacher in France.

3 ____ The writer and Dong Hua have been friends for about two years.

4 ____ Dong Hua has been in three TV dramas so far.

E Based on the passage in (D), circle the most appropriate choice. INTERPRETIVE

1 Which of the following is true about Dong Hua's tutoring?

  a One of his students is a famous actor.

  b The son of one of his students is a famous actor.

  c The father of one of his students is a famous actor.

2 Which of the following is true about Dong Hua's performance in his first TV appearance?

  a He quickly overcame his initial nervousness despite his lack of acting experience.

  b He succeeded even though his lack of acting experience made the director nervous initially.

  c The director and crew were happy with his work as a language tutor.

在中国长期生活的外国人主要有两种。第一种人很多，他们在大学当教授或者在公司里当管理人员，工作稳定，收入都比较高。这种人虽然工作也会有压力，但是生活一般都过得很舒服。另外一种人是自由职业者，他们有时候当翻译，有时候做家教，有时候当导游，有时候当演员。这种人因为有时有工作，有时没工作，所以收入不太稳定。但是因为中国的东西一般都比较便宜，所以他们的生活还是没问题的。更重要的是，他们能认识很多中国老百姓，交很多朋友，所以比教授和管理人员更容易融入中国社会。在这两种外国人中，第二种人挣钱挣得比较少，可是他们往往比第一种人更了解中国的生活。

在中國長期生活的外國人主要有兩種。第一種人很多，他們在大學當教授或者在公司裡當管理人員，工作穩定，收入都比較高。這種人雖然工作也會有壓力，但是生活一般都過得很舒服。另外一種人是自由職業者，他們有時候當翻譯，有時候做家教，有時候當導遊，有時候當演員。這種人因為有時有工作，有時沒工作，所以收入不太穩定。但是因為中國的東西一般都比較便宜，所以他們的生活還是沒問題的。更重要的是，他們能認識很多中國老百姓，交很多朋友，所以比教授和管理人員更容易融入中國社會。在這兩種外國人中，第二種人掙錢掙得比較少，可是他們往往比第一種人更了解中國的生活。

1 ____ This passage is about international students in China.

2 ____ According to the passage, foreigners in China who have a stable income usually live a stress-free life.

3 ____ Foreigners who are freelance professionals in China often live on the fringes of Chinese society.

G Based on the passage in (F), circle the most appropriate choice. INTERPRETIVE

1 According to the passage, foreigners who are freelance professionals in China often work as

a managers, translators, tutors, and actors.

b translators, professors, actors, and tour guides.

c tutors, tour guides, actors, and translators.

H Look at this photo and answer the question in English. INTERPRETIVE

Who is the advertiser seeking?_____

I Look at this advertisement and answer the question in English. INTERPRETIVE

这是什么广告？他们卖什么？请用英文写出两样。
這是什麼廣告？他們賣什麼？請用英文寫出兩樣。

_____

_____

A Form a character by combining the given components as indicated. Then use that character to write a word, phrase, or short sentence.

1 左边一个"小区"的"区"，右边一个"欠钱"的"欠"，

   左邊一個"小區"的"區"，右邊一個"欠錢"的"欠"，

   是 ＿＿＿＿＿＿ 的 ＿＿＿ 。

2 左边一个三点水，右边一个"加州"的"州"，

   左邊一個三點水，右邊一個"加州"的"州"，

   是 ＿＿＿＿＿＿ 的 ＿＿＿ 。

3 左边一个提手旁，右边一个"高楼"的"高"，

   左邊一個提手旁，右邊一個"高樓"的"高"，

   是 ＿＿＿＿＿＿ 的 ＿＿＿ 。

4 左边一个"木"，右边一个"交通"的"交"，

   左邊一個"木"，右邊一個"交通"的"交"，

   是 ＿＿＿＿＿＿ 的 ＿＿＿ 。

5 左边一个言字旁，右边一个"便宜"的"宜"，

   左邊一個言字旁，右邊一個"便宜"的"宜"，

   是 ＿＿＿＿＿＿ 的 ＿＿＿ 。

B Use 把 to list options for managing money. PRESENTATIONAL

1 depositing the money in the bank

＿＿＿＿＿＿＿＿＿＿＿＿＿＿＿＿＿＿＿＿＿＿＿＿＿＿＿＿＿＿＿＿＿＿＿＿＿

2 investing the money in the stock market

＿＿＿＿＿＿＿＿＿＿＿＿＿＿＿＿＿＿＿＿＿＿＿＿＿＿＿＿＿＿＿＿＿＿＿＿＿

3 giving the money to your parents

_____

4 lending the money to your classmate

_____

5 placing the money under your bed

_____

6 spending all the money

_____

C Complete the following exchanges. Use 而已 to give understated answers, following the example below. INTERPERSONAL

Person A: 听说你炒股，赔了一些钱。 (two hundred)
          聽說你炒股，賠了一些錢。

Person B: 不多，只赔了两百块钱而已。
          不多，只賠了兩百塊錢而已。

1 Person A: 看你买这么多菜，今天晚上你请几个人来吃火
              锅？ (five people)
              看你買這麼多菜，今天晚上你請幾個人來吃火
              鍋？

   Person B: 没请多少人，_____。
              沒請多少人，_____。

2 Person A: 你一会儿搞翻译，一会儿搞推销，一会儿又当
              家教，你到底有几份工作啊？不累啊？ (three jobs)
              你一會兒搞翻譯，一會兒搞推銷，一會兒又當
              家教，你到底有幾份工作啊？不累啊？

   Person B: 不累，_____。
              不累，_____。

3 Person A: 你对这个城市这么了解，在这儿已经待了很长一段时间了吧。 (half a year)

你對這個城市這麼了解，在這兒已經待了很長一段時間了吧。

Person B: 不长，＿＿＿＿＿＿＿＿＿＿＿＿＿＿＿＿＿＿＿。

不長，＿＿＿＿＿＿＿＿＿＿＿＿＿＿＿＿＿＿＿。

D Translate these sentences into Chinese using 在⋯下. PRESENTATIONAL

1 With help from colleagues, she got used to her new job very quickly.

＿＿＿＿＿＿＿＿＿＿＿＿＿＿＿＿＿＿＿＿＿＿＿＿＿＿＿

2 Under the guidance (教导/教導) of his professor, he got his master's degree without a hitch.

＿＿＿＿＿＿＿＿＿＿＿＿＿＿＿＿＿＿＿＿＿＿＿＿＿＿＿

3 Persuaded by his parents, he decided not to invest in the stock market.

＿＿＿＿＿＿＿＿＿＿＿＿＿＿＿＿＿＿＿＿＿＿＿＿＿＿＿

E Translate these dialogues into Chinese. PRESENTATIONAL

1 Person A: Thank you for your help. If you hadn't contacted that TV station, they wouldn't have let me act in that TV drama.

＿＿＿＿＿＿＿＿＿＿＿＿＿＿＿＿＿＿＿＿＿＿＿＿＿＿＿

＿＿＿＿＿＿＿＿＿＿＿＿＿＿＿＿＿＿＿＿＿＿＿＿＿＿＿

Person B: I simply made a phone call.

＿＿＿＿＿＿＿＿＿＿＿＿＿＿＿＿＿＿＿＿＿＿＿＿＿＿＿

2 Person A: How was the situation in terms of sales of solar panels and energy-efficient batteries last month?

＿＿＿＿＿＿＿＿＿＿＿＿＿＿＿＿＿＿＿＿＿＿＿＿＿＿＿

＿＿＿＿＿＿＿＿＿＿＿＿＿＿＿＿＿＿＿＿＿＿＿＿＿＿＿

Person B: Under your leadership, we became one of the three biggest companies for solar panels and energy-efficient batteries in the world. The more we market and promote our products, the more our sales thrive.

_____

_____

_____

Person A: Wonderful. We should get together tonight to celebrate.

_____

Person B: I'm all for it! (I raise both hands to support this proposal.)

_____

F Translate these passages into Chinese. PRESENTATIONAL

1 Classmates, thank you for hosting this farewell dinner for me. Who knew that four years of college life would go by so quickly? Tomorrow I'll fly back to Spain. When I came to China, I didn't know a word of Chinese. Because everyone often helped and took care of me, I've lived these four years in China very happily. Every day I see and hear something new. I'll never forget (all these things). I also have to thank Teacher Bai for teaching me so many things. Come, let's toast to our friendship! The world is getting smaller. I welcome everyone to come see me in Spain.

_____

_____

_____

_____

_____

_____

_____

2   Pepe (裴佩) *(Péi Pèi)* and I were roommates for four years, so I have to say a few words. The school asked me to help Pepe learn Chinese, but I feel that I've learned a lot of things from Pepe as well. Pepe is good at time-management. The reason I am so healthy today is because no matter how busy we were with schoolwork (学习/學習), every weekend Pepe made me go to the soccer field with him to play soccer. He made me realize that health and schoolwork are equally important. I'll never forget you, Pepe. Now let's invite Teacher Bai to say a few words.

_____

_____

_____

_____

_____

_____

_____

3   Pepe, I want to first congratulate you on finding a great job. Has Pepe told everyone that he's found a job with a Chinese company in Spain? I heard that Pepe wasn't nervous at all during the interview. He performed very well. The manager who interviewed him believed in Pepe's ability and felt he has many strengths. I'm really happy for him. Pepe, I wish you a safe journey tomorrow and a successful career.

_____

_____

_____

_____

_____

_____

_____

4   Today was my first day at work. Next month I'll go to Europe on a business trip to promote our company's solar panels and energy-efficient batteries. Our company's products are excellent and affordable. Besides, they are good for the environment, so they sell extremely well. I have three schoolmates at our company. They say they will take care of me. I'll call my mom this weekend to tell her that my work will go without a hitch and ask her to stop worrying.

_____

_____

_____

_____

_____

5   My schoolmate Wang Ziming (王子明) has been working at the company for three years after graduating from college. He says that although the work is very interesting, there is also a lot of pressure. Sometimes he has to stay up late. He is really quite impressive, having become the manager of the international sales department at such a young age. Not only does he understand sales, but he is also a great manager. The only thing is that I think he needs to pay more attention to rest. I hope he can take a trip to relax a little bit from time to time.

_____

_____

_____

_____

_____

_____

_____

G   A classmate in your Chinese class is graduating at the end of the semester. What would you write on a graduation card or a banner for a send-off party to wish him/her great future success?

PRESENTATIONAL

H You've become acquainted with the characters of IC3 and IC4 for over a year now. Create a personal bio for your favorite character. Include basic information about his/her upbringing, hobbies, interests, personality, education, work experience, future aspirations, strengths, flaws, etc. Compared with when you were first introduced to him/her, what is he/she like now? What has he/she seen, done, and learned? Are you and the character alike in any way? PRESENTATIONAL

I Write a story in Chinese based on the four images below. Make sure that your story has a beginning, middle, and end, and that the transition from one picture to the next is smooth and logical. PRESENTATIONAL

1

2

3

4

Bringing It Together (Lessons 16–20)

A Write down the correct pronunciation, including tones, of the following short sentences in *pinyin*. Use a computer or smartphone to record yourself speaking. If you've been asked to do so, send the recording to your teacher. Then translate each sentence into English. INTERPRETIVE

1 新鲜、不受污染的空气有益于身体健康。

新鮮、不受汙染的空氣有益於身體健康。

_____

_____

2 风能、水能、太阳能都是绿色能源。

風能、水能、太陽能都是綠色能源。

_____

_____

3 政府规定，夏天公共场所的空调温度不可低于摄氏
26度。

政府規定，夏天公共場所的空調溫度不可低於攝氏
26度。

_____

_____

4 很多退休老人把自己辛辛苦苦省下来的钱，拿去投资
风险较大的股市。

很多退休老人把自己辛辛苦苦省下來的錢，拿去投資
風險較大的股市。

_____

_____

5 最近的世界经济危机，引起很多人对自己的理财方式进行思考。

最近的世界經濟危機，引起很多人對自己的理財方式進行思考。

_____

_____

6 他说服妻子把存款从银行拿出来，好好享受生活。

他说服妻子把存款從銀行拿出來，好好享受生活。

_____

_____

_____

7 "有朋自远方来，不亦乐乎"这句话有两千多年的历史。

"有朋自遠方來，不亦樂乎"這句話有兩千多年的歷史。

_____

_____

8 秦始皇对中国文字的统一有贡献，但他修坟墓、修宫殿、杀读书人、烧古书，也引起老百姓对他的不满。

秦始皇對中國文字的統一有貢獻，但他修墳墓、修宮殿、殺讀書人、燒古書，也引起老百姓對他的不滿。

_____

_____

_____

9 中国历史非常长，曾经是科技发达，技术先进的文明古国。

中國歷史非常長，曾經是科技發達，技術先進的文明古國。

---

10 他取得博士学位，从海外归来，今天去一家跨国公司面试。他对自己的表现很不满意，觉得很郁闷。

他取得博士學位，從海外歸來，今天去一家跨國公司面試。他對自己的表現很不滿意，覺得很鬱悶。

---

11 那位总经理虽然有些严肃，但大家都同意他是个管理人材。

那位總經理雖然有些嚴肅，但大家都同意他是個管理人材。

---

12 收到录用通知时，他的脸上马上多云转晴，笑了起来。

收到錄用通知時，他的臉上馬上多雲轉晴，笑了起來。

13 每周工作聚会时，他都希望经理、同事告诉他自己的优缺点。

每週工作聚會時，他都希望經理、同事告訴他自己的優缺點。

_____

_____

14 她是一位很好的演员，而且善于推销新产品，很多公司都找她拍广告，最近特别火。

她是一位很好的演員，而且善於推銷新產品，很多公司都找她拍廣告，最近特別火。

_____

_____

_____

_____

_____

15 他要移民去欧洲，朋友们给他饯行，大家为友谊干杯，互祝身体健康，生活幸福，事业成功。

他要移民去歐洲，朋友們給他餞行，大家為友誼乾杯，互祝身體健康，生活幸福，事業成功。

_____

_____

_____

_____

_____

A While studying abroad in China, you run into the following scenarios. PRESENTATIONAL

1 Suppose you want to share your knowledge about how people conserve energy and protect the environment in your own country. What would you say?

节能/節能   环保/環保

_____   _____

_____   _____

_____   _____

_____   _____

_____   _____

_____   _____

2 Suppose you want to share some basic strategies for financial planning and investment. What would you suggest?

理财/理財   投资/投資

_____   _____

_____   _____

_____   _____

_____   _____

_____   _____

3 Suppose you want to demonstrate your knowledge of Chinese history. What dynasties or historical figures would you mention and what would you say about the roles your chosen historical figures played?

朝代   历史人物/歷史人物

_____   _____

_____   _____

_____   _____

_____   _____

4 Suppose you are talking with your new friends about why you have come to China and how you see yourself adapting to life in China. What sorts of things would you mention?

什么吸引你来中国留学或者工作？

什麼吸引你來中國留學或者工作？

_____

_____

_____

_____

你怎么能很快地适应中国的生活？

你怎麼能很快地適應中國的生活？

_____

_____

_____

_____

5 Suppose you are planning to see off a Chinese friend who is going to work in your country and welcoming someone from your country who has just arrived in China to study Chinese. What wishes would you express for each occasion?

饯行/餞行   接风/接風

_____   _____

_____   _____

_____   _____

A Describe three things that you do on a daily basis to save energy and reduce your carbon footprint, with your most frequent habit listed first. PRESENTATIONAL

1 _____

2 _____

3 _____

B Describe three good practices that will help you achieve your financial goals, with the least risky and/or most helpful listed first. PRESENTATIONAL

1 _____

2 _____

3 _____

C Describe three things that you can do to make a good impression when you are on a job interview, with the most important listed first. PRESENTATIONAL

1 _____

2 _____

3 _____

D Describe three events from Chinese history that are impressive to you and why, with the most impressive listed first. PRESENTATIONAL

1 _____

2 _____

3 _____

E Describe three ways to integrate into Chinese society, with the most important listed first.

1 _____

2 _____

3 _____

IV. Summarize and Report

A Interview your Chinese teacher and Chinese international students on campus and ask for their advice for students like you who wish to study or work in China. Organize your notes and write a simple report based on your interviews. Include advice on food, housing, commuting, budgeting, shopping, internship and job opportunities, and some basic essential facts about Chinese geography and history. INTERPERSONAL & PRESENTATIONAL